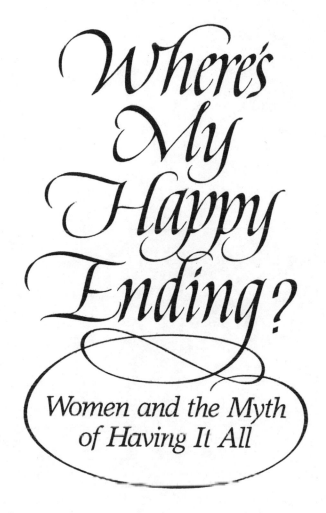

Where's My Happy Ending?

Women and the Myth of Having It All

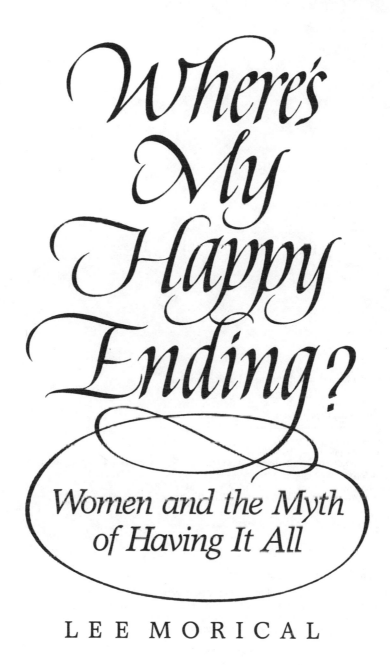

Where's My Happy Ending?

Women and the Myth of Having It All

LEE MORICAL

Addison-Wesley Publishing Company
Reading, Massachusetts • Menlo Park, California
Wokingham, Berkshire • Amsterdam • Don Mills, Ontario • Sydney

Library of Congress Cataloging in Publication Data

Morical, Lee.
  Where's my happy ending?

  Bibliography: p.
  Includes index.
    1. Women — United States — Psychology.   2.   Women — United States — Social
conditions.   3.   Self-perception.   I.   Title.
HQ1426.M856   1984   305.4'2   84-14539
ISBN 0-201-14052-7

Cover design by Marshall Henrichs
Text design by Diana Eames Esterly
Set in 11 point Korinna by Compset, Inc.

ISBN 0-201-14052-7

ABCDEFGHIJ-DO-8654

Acknowledgments

The completion of the writing of a book does not call for modesty; from beginning to end one has been painfully alone in front of the stack of blank paper.

Yet there are those others whose contributions have been in some way so important that it is hard to imagine that the book could ever have been begun or completed without them. These I here acknowledge with thanks:

My friend, the late Roselyn Milavitz, for never letting me forget that I am a writer; author Alice Lake, whose own sensitive writing about my work provided much of the impetus for this task; my student and friend, Shirley Mangelson, for her consistent faith and encouragement; John Williams, associate professor of human development and colleague at the University of Wisconsin—Stout, whose hard questions helped me formulate the book's focus, and Jack Biersdorf, director of the Institute for Advanced Pastoral Studies and beloved teacher, for helping me toss away the key to that prison called "perfection."

I thank also David Zimmerman for believing in my work enough to share his agent with me; Connie Clausen, David's agent and mine, for never letting me retreat into the comfort of my doubts; and Guy Kettelhack, Connie's associate, for his ability to give world-class critique with the ultimate in graciousness and perception. Appreciation also to

Doe Coover, vice-president of the General Books Division of Addison-Wesley and the other women of that division, and to Linda Sunshine, my editor, for the clarity of their thinking in the initial planning of this work and for their interest throughout.

Special thanks to my husband, Edward, for all the reasons he knows so well; to my sisters and brothers in Diakrisis, and to Nomes for his comfort throughout all the weary days.

Most of all I thank Mary Anderson, my assistant and my friend, who believed in me, kept at me, listened to me, typed for me, and in no small sense, made it happen.

How do I know that the world is like this?
Because of what is within me.

Lao-tzu

*In thanksgiving for the gifts
of the journey*

Contents

INTRODUCTION   xi

1   *New Dreams, Old Awakenings: Where Did It All Go Wrong?*   1

2   *Working Your Way to Oblivion*   15

3   *The Invisible Housewife*   33

4   *The New Depression*   51

5   *The Beautiful Sound of Silence*   69

6   *Finding Your Balance*   91

7   *Flowing with Life*   111

8   *Race to Nowhere, Journey to Everywhere*   127

9   *Making Choices and Letting Go*   147

10   *Living Your Happy Ending*   165

REFERENCES   171

INDEX   173

Introduction

It stood out in the pile of mail on my desk. "Women have arrived," it blared in orange Day-Glo. "They have scaled mountains, become priests, gone to work in coal mines [!], gained entry into the executive suite. Women have indeed arrived!"

I looked for the punch line, the disclaimer at the end, but there was none. The flyer was announcing a conference at a prestigious university to celebrate the "arrival" of women.

I didn't know whether to laugh or to cry. On my desk that day were more than fifty letters, adding to the thousands I'd received already that spring from women all over the country in response to my recent appearance on a national television program and a story about my work in a woman's magazine and the thousands more that already stuffed my files.

The letters came from coal boomtowns in Wyoming and from Iowa and from all up and down the East Coast and, heavily, from New Jersey and California. They came from secretaries and full-time housewives and real estate saleswomen and account executives. They came from wives of ministers and construction workers and lawyers and businessmen from places as diverse as Grosse Pointe, Michigan, and Yazoo City, Mississippi. The farthest came from an American woman stationed with her husband in Germany, the closest from a woman who lives two streets away. The letters reflected great reservoirs of talent, good humor, compassion—and unhappiness. Most of the letters were from women who had not only not arrived but were not even sure where it was they wanted to go. Other women wrote that they had "arrived" but, now that they are there, find it an exhausting and unfulfilling place.

The letters spoke of confusion and alienation from what their writers perceived to be the media version of "today's woman."

"We don't want to go back to the old way of being a woman," they said, "but the new way isn't working much better. Where do we fit?"

It has been fifteen years since the August I knew that I was going to spend the next part of my life helping women realize that they had not been born to "fit" someone else's idea of who they should be.

After two years as a journalist and editor I'd spent ten more as a full-time housewife and was now several years into my work as writer-editor of a university news service. Although I was back in the profession for which I'd been trained, I knew there was something more I was to do with my life. I had no idea what it was to be, but then, recuperating from surgery that summer in Utah while my husband attended graduate school and my children did the summer things children do, I allowed myself to take the time to stop, think, and listen. Before August ended I knew that I was to make something redemptive of my own experiences, which, though their pain had healed, would always be a part of me, and I was to do this by sharing them in some way with others.

In the fall of 1969 I began working on my master's degree in counseling. I still remember my first two clients: a 22-year-old unmarried woman who was pregnant by a man she didn't love but with whom she had "made" love because she didn't want to lose him, and a 62-year-old housewife who said her whole life was slipping away without anything ever having happened.

In the years since then there have been hundreds of classrooms and church basements and pulpits and head tables and microphones and television cameras. But mostly there have been the women, the thousands with whom I've worked as a teacher and a therapist in lecture halls and workshops, in my office and their living rooms, over tea, beer, textbooks, diaper bags, and briefcases. There has been, in the stories of these women, much pain, but there has also been the reflection of tremendous growth.

By 1980 I felt the energy, as I traveled back and forth across the country, of women who were beginning at last to value themselves. A year later, recuperating again from surgery, immersed in research and teaching, involved with colleagues who felt as I did, I had reached the point of believing, along with so many others, that the majority of women in the United States *had* arrived—were, in fact, well on their way to finding lives of fulfillment. But then I began to travel and lecture again, and then came the Donahue show and the *Woman's Day* interview, and I was deluged with the thousands of letters which showed me that our assumptions had not been correct. They showed me, in painful and poignant stories, what all of us should have known but wanted so much not to know: women do not "arrive," as if on a boxcar marked "Happiness Express." They must come, as we have always known, one by one, each in her own time and through her own pain and growth. And if a woman has not reached a point of strength where she is able to withstand it, she will be open to the distortion of dreams as much in this time as in any other decade.

This book has been formed in part by some of my personal and professional experiences, but mostly it has sprung from the words of all the women with whom I've spent the past fifteen years, the ones with whom I've wept and danced. I have agonized at times that because of the volume of mail I have not been able to respond to each of the letters and phone calls and requests.

And so my response is this book. It is not very much about why things are the way they are, because to ask why is to presuppose that there is an answer. And for many of the things in our lives there are no answers. Instead, this book is about the way things are. It is about things you already know but perhaps do not realize you know. You have just let other voices shout so loudly you can't hear your own. You have not trusted your own truth and your own answers. This book is about you and for you because I have been with you and I am you. The telling of it may help you on your own journey. I don't know. What matters is that we each keep on with our journeys and that we realize that we are not alone in them.

Menomonie, Wisconsin
May 1984

Happiness does not exclude pain and grief
but only depression and a sense of
worthlessness; it can grow from the former
as it is destroyed by the latter.

Erich Fromm

1

New Dreams, Old Awakenings: Where Did It All Go Wrong?

A vibrant 32-year-old in Boston tells me that she is thinking seriously of chucking her job in public relations and taking a part-time job in a boutique so she can have some time to breathe.

A mother of two teenagers who works part time in a New Jersey suburb writes, "I'm depressed but I'm ashamed to admit it. All the other women I know seem to have gotten it all together."

On the same day that an Iowa woman writes, "I'm only 25, married, two kids, but already life has passed me by," I hear from a woman in San Antonio who says she is tired of being made to feel stupid for staying home to raise her kids. "No one," she says, "understands."

And in Detroit, a 55-year-old woman tells me how she regrets having divorced her husband. "I was trying to find myself," she says, "but the only thing I found was a big empty space. Where do I go from here?"

Although separated by geography and income and age, the women's stories, like most of those I hear, contain a common thread: I did it right. I followed the instructions. I did what I thought would make it work. I used my talents/got a job/stayed home/married the right guy/divorced the wrong one/tried to find myself.

And although no one says the words out loud, not too far below the surface is the poignant other part that silently finishes the sentence, that eternal wondering expectation: "And so where's my happy ending?"

Women today are bombarded with the message that they are living in the best of times for women, but for many of them it doesn't feel like it. The smug face of the slim woman in the blazer who has multiple orgasms and bakes whole wheat bread in her spare time haunts them. Unwilling to retreat to the old ways of being a woman, knowing they can't stand still and survive with any dignity, they've tried the new ways of being a woman only to find that there is still pain.

"If I can't make it now, in the best of times," many ask, "if I've tried all the how-to's and have still blown it—what kind of nothing am I?"

Each struggles on, feeling more and more frustrated, but carefully hiding both the struggle and the frustration because everyone else seems to be doing just fine.

Real progress has been made during the past decade in the areas of male-female relationships, education, and the workplace. Consciousness has been raised on the part of both men and women. Both can and do work outside the home: dust rags, we have belatedly discovered, have no gender. Women can and do drive trucks, men can and do answer telephones and clean bedpans. Yet despite this apparent progress, the women I talk with and hear from convince me that for many women the changes are not as real, as widespread—or as satisfying—as they appear on the surface.

- Women who used to feel exhausted shagging little kids all day now drop their weary bods into bed after a day at the office and wonder where it all went wrong.

- Women who chose a career instead of motherhood now face the biological time clock and find themselves dreaming about having time to bake bread or read a book all the way through.

- The woman who still dares call herself "housewife" finds that she has disappeared from the television screen, the magazine pages, and the concern of the American public: she is demographically dead (and, if she has little children, she also dreams of having time to bake bread or read a book all the way through).

- The woman who has taken courses in everything from assertiveness training to zen meditation wonders again why she can't take off fifteen pounds or get her husband to talk with her.

And all of them, according to a recent survey by *Better Homes and Gardens,* see themselves as responsible for all the household chores!

For many of us, the changes of the past twenty years did provide options that made possible the creation of fulfilled lives. Other women, already content in their lives, went on living them.

But millions of women fall into a third group, a group caught in a frustrating and painful ambivalence.

Who Are These Women?

"Who are all these women who keep calling and writing to you?" A counselor colleague of mine is sincerely puzzled. He is tall, lean—a runner—and sensitive. But he sees women today as having it "all together," and he cannot understand that women anywhere still have any questions about much of anything.

It's hard to write or talk about these women because, on the surface, each appears to be so different from the others. What can a housewife with three children in Cherry Hills have in common with a sales rep in Pittsburgh who is wondering whether to have a baby or not? Can a 26-year-old woman who is a third-year law student at the University of Minnesota really share any of the sense of loneliness of the homemaker from Kansas City who is returning to school at forty-one to begin her first course toward a B.A. in psychology?

They can and they do, but neither they nor many others believe it because they seem so diverse. They aren't a discrete group. They can't be labeled. They aren't disabled or disadvantaged or displaced or dying. As one woman wrote to me, "I've got too much to be considered destitute, and I'm too poor to be solvent. I'm too intelligent to get much sympathy, and I'm not clever enough to solve my own problems!" They are instead that amorphous group known variously as middle class, working wife, housewife, homemaker, mother-to-be, or mother-who-may-choose-not-to-be. They may have a high school education or a master's degree or beyond. They may be 21 or 67, and they may work as a clerk or the president of their own business, or they may not work outside of their homes at all.

But what they all have in common is a sense that their lives are not coming out quite the way they had expected. Despite their attempts to find the answer, despite their own best efforts, somehow, somewhere along the line, something went wrong. And they share the sense that, if things continue to go as they have been, there may never be a happy ending.

The Other Side of the Rainbow

"No one believes in happy endings anymore," a friend informs me when I tell her what this book is going to be titled.

I would have agreed with her once, but I don't anymore.

On a sticky summer evening in 1971 an overweight woman in her late twenties sat in my office in a pink sweatshirt staring at the soggy, torn Kleenex she was twisting in her hands.

"I have everything I always thought I wanted: a husband, two healthy kids, a nice house. So why don't I ever feel happy anymore?"

I still remember thinking she must be an aberration, a leftover from the decade before, in the days when such stories had been common and when I had undergone my own struggle for equilibrium. Surely I couldn't be hearing this now in 1971, when women were beginning to have choices? But I was hearing it, and it is a story I have not stopped hearing to this day.

Women's expectations of a happy ending did not die when they stopped believing that they should "save" themselves for a special man, polish the silver every Saturday, or knit favors for their children's birthday parties. Fostered in us from the storybooks of our childhood, nurtured by the records and magazines of our teen years, and fanned to fruition by the books, movies, and advertisements that surround us all of our lives, the happy ending is as much with us now as it was when my aunt Emma lovingly opened her first bar of Pear's soap in 1904.

Since the beginning of the twentieth century, when even the thought of happy endings first began to be a possibility for real, live, ordinary folk, there has been no shortage of people to tell us what that ending should be and how to get there, no shortage of scenarios available to women to get them to the desired goal. But too often, the scenarios have been designed to be played out against a background of contrived sets, jerry-built for the year or the decade. Only after a woman has learned her lines and gotten into her costume and stepped onstage has she learned, to her dismay and pain, that behind the set is only another mortal cranking out a story that promises to put her on the other side of the rainbow but instead dumps her into an alien land totally out of touch with the reality of her own life.

It's not called "happy ending" anymore, of course, unless it is spoken of with bemused nostalgia—we're not that naive!—and yet it remains, deep in our bones and in our psyches. Today it is called "success."

There is nothing wrong with believing in happy endings or in success. In fact, it can be fun. It can give your life direction, can even give you something to think about when you are at the dentist's. Where the trouble begins is

1. When you let someone else decide what your happy ending (success) will be

2. When you let someone else decide how you will get to it

3.   When you start believing that there is only one "right" happy
     ending and one "right" way to get there

4.   When you let the goal of getting to your happy ending
     (success) become more important than the journey

In each part of the twentieth century women have, with great
hope, played out their prescribed scenarios and, when these have failed
to bring the promised happiness, have asked what went wrong. When,
in the 1920s, a woman could not get her breasts flattened enough or
her father to spring for a college education, she felt a failure. When, in
the 1950s, she could not get her laundry to whiten and her copper to
sparkle and her kids and her zoysia plugs to grow an inch a month, she
knew she must be doing something wrong. And now, in the 1980s,
when she cannot immediately pick from among the array of options
open to her, cannot handle job-home-husband-children-hobbies-health-
hair with aplomb, she entertains a nagging sense that if she just tried
harder, she could make it.

Intrinsic in these "decade answers" is the notion that there is a
right answer, a prescription which, if followed, will bring about the happy
ending.

In the 1950s the answers that had been designed to help
women live happily ever after had to do with a three-bedroom home in
the suburbs, a husband, three children, a dog, and a Whirlpool washer
and dryer. Because of my own belief that "they" had the answers (the
whole world, wasn't it?), I thought I must have misread the instructions
when I felt scared and smothered by this scenario. My daughters laugh
at this scenario now and at my naiveté, and yet how different was my
belief then from that of a woman today who thinks that she is out of step
not to want the vice-presidency of sales when it is offered, even if it
means leaving her husband in Dallas and their kids in a day-care center
for the next five years?

It is obvious to most of us now that a life in which women have
options is far better than a life in which they, apparently, had none. But
any life in which a person feels she or he must follow someone else's
script is as bad as the next, no matter how full of opportunities it is.
There is nothing wrong with having a husband and a child or two or
three or eleven, a Whirlpool, a vice-presidency, a home in the suburbs,

or day-care centers. What is wrong is the expectation that any one of these things will, *de facto,* provide us with more happiness than any of the others. If you have any doubt that the happiness one of these things is supposed to provide is not the happiness you want, then run—don't walk—away from it. If you don't, you will become a prisoner of that "happiness" no matter how good it is said to be.

For some women, the notion of a happy ending is not so much a preference as it is a mandate. It becomes a life goal. They were raised to believe that they would not get their cream puff until they'd eaten their brussels sprouts, could not go to the movies until the dishes were done. Unable to enjoy the journey to their goal, too driven to stop at the oases along the way, they spend their entire lives "doing it right." Look the right way, join the right club, wear the right outfit, marry the right person, find the right career ladder, run the right number of miles, lose the right number of pounds, and always, always have a skin and sunset that are forever radiant. Once done with this task, you will then have reached the goal.

But if you think of your goal as a happy *ending* and success only as a prize to be worked for or earned in the future, you doom yourself not only to failure but to unhappiness. For when you live life so rigidly that you never allow yourself to savor your cream puff until you have swallowed your brussels sprouts, you miss the discovery that happiness is to be experienced *now*—not only after a life well lived, but during each day of it.

The Distortion of the Dream

When I began my work with women in the late 1960s, the old expectations were still very firmly in place. It was still widely accepted that tending to husband and children was the direct route to happiness for every woman. Work outside the home had to be gotten out of the way before marriage (when I went back to work after my youngest child entered kindergarten, a neighbor told me I was putting my entire family at risk). The best way to handle controversy was silence, and the best thing to wear to the Rotary Club dinner dance was something neat but not noticeable.

There was a horrifying dependency on others—usually husband and children—for one's happiness, and over all hung an almost palpable sense of joylessness.

Changes began to take place in the early 1970s, as they do in every decade, and as a result of these changes it seemed that we women were entering a time in which we could at last make some real choices for ourselves. It looked at last to be a time when a woman could stay home or work outside of it, could bake bread or do brain surgery, and that from this everyone would benefit.

For many women this is exactly what happened; the promise was fulfilled. But for many others—and for many reasons—it never worked out that way, and the marvelous new potential for real choice got lost as women began to exchange one set of expectations for another. Women who had been told, and had once believed, that all happiness resides within the home now were told, and believed, that all happiness lies outside of it: going to work became one of the new decade's "answers."

There is a historical phenomenon that occurs when long-held traditions begin to change rapidly: an inordinate value is placed upon anything new. The new becomes automatically "good"; it is new, therefore it is good, therefore I must do it. For the woman who has simply exchanged old decade answers for new, or the young woman who has bought the expectations of this decade, the prison remains and the key that will provide release is as elusive as ever.

Sometimes, in interviews, I am asked what I see to be the biggest problems facing women today. I never have to guess because women continue to tell me: too much to do, too many choices, not feeling good about themselves, guilt, loneliness, confusion, depression.

Intrinsic in these problems are the new expectations, spawned once again by a belief that there is a "right" answer and born of the eternal desire to find one's happy ending.

Today's Expectations, Yesterday's Disappointments

The new expectations are, in large part, very natural reactions to, and corrections of, the old. They represent years of hard work. They have come to us, as have their counterparts in preceding decades, by a sort of cultural osmosis. They are, in a very real sense, "in the air." Because today's expectations are so intrinsically good and because they make so much sense and because they are so pervasive, it soon becomes almost impossible to deny them. Even when you feel that you do not agree, you become convinced that to disagree is to be hopelessly out of touch or ungrateful or both. Taken to, but not beyond, their logical conclusions, they provide good starting points for a satisfying life. But when they are taken too far, they become in their own ways as deadly as their predecessors.

What are these new expectations? How have we allowed them, in their own ways, to let us down when they promised us so much?

Expectation # 1: Getting a Job Is the Answer

For so long women had to choose between working at a paying job or working as a wife and mother that it is no wonder it felt like died-and-gone-to-heaven time for us when we reached the point of being able to choose one or both of the above and even, on occasion, get the egg roll, too. But now a 28-year-old Minneapolis woman tells me she became an attorney because her mother, 53, had been "bored" with being a house-wife, yet her dissatisfaction level is about where her mother's was in 1958. "I'd give anything to stay home with my baby daughter," she said, "but my mother insists I'll be bored, too." A secretary in Illinois told me recently that the only thing that kept her going for the last five years be-fore her last child was in school was the knowledge that she'd be able to get a job. "Now I hate every minute of it. I feel swallowed alive with all the demands on my time and energy. There's no time for anything but work, but I can't afford to quit." The clean toilet bowl has been replaced as a sign of success by the sales contract, and thousands of women are wondering why the same old frustrations, tiredness, chest pain, and lone-liness continue. Without support from others, women are finding that life in the trenches of office, school, hospital, or restaurant is about as much fun as four o'clock on a rainy afternoon with all the kids home from school. Others, tired of living the job twenty-four hours a day, are choos-ing to stay home.

Expectation #2: Staying Home Is the Answer

Inside the letter is a wallet-sized picture of an attractive blond woman in her twenties. The face has been X'ed out with a heavy black marker. "This is how I used to look," the letter says. "I saw how tired my mom always was trying to work and take care of us, so I decided when I got married I'd stay home full time. Now I have everything I thought I wanted, and I don't feel I'm worth a thing. No one could take a picture of me anymore because I'm not here." From a Connecticut suburb a woman of 53 sends me her description of herself: "Married, two children, nice home, plenty of money, miserable." The old expectation of being fulfilled by marriage, babies, and the chance to be taken care of disappeared for a decade but has returned as the new expectation of being fulfilled by marriage, babies, and the chance to get out of the rat race. Women in their twenties are buying into the promise of marriage again, women in their thirties are retiring to motherhood, and all of them, like the 40- and 50-year-olds before them, are finding that there are still thistles in paradise.

Expectation #3: With So Many Options, I Won't Get Depressed

In class one day, one of my students, a woman of 39, raised a question that puzzles many women today. "I understand why I used to get so depressed when I was home all the time. I always felt sort of helpless, as if I'd be trapped there forever. I thought things would be different after my divorce and when I went back to work, but they aren't." A recurrent myth is that women who have choices won't get depressed. But since depression is an enigmatic illness that affects mind, body, and spirit, it can happen any time our lives get out of balance, whether we are at home or on the job. Since loss is one of the prime triggers of depression, women who feel a loss of stability because of the large number of life choices open to them can succumb to a "new" depression that feels exactly the same as the "old" depression experienced by their mothers or themselves.

Expectation #4: Talking It Out Will Improve Every Relationship

The belief that talking it over is the answer to every relationship is beginning to boomerang, and many women are getting hit. Talking it over has
real value when partners in a relationship share similar communication
patterns, but forcing communication between two people—husband
and wife, mother and daughter—who do not share the same patterns
can be devastating. Forcing noncommunicative husbands into marriage-enrichment weekends, insisting that the entire family have a night
of "sharing," and sitting around with other women endlessly airing problems are not turning out to produce the positive results that we had all
once hoped for. For many women, the question of whether they talk too
much or not enough is no longer the most productive one. More important, often, is the question: Does it need to be said at all?

Expectation #5: I Won't Be Taken Seriously If I Show I Care

For so long women have explained and apologized for not being good
enough that we may heave a collective sigh of relief that those days are
now over. But are they? As old patterns give way to new, a new batch of
insecurities fly into the vacuum. In an attempt to be perceived as strong,
many women feel compelled to apologize and explain away their feelings of caring for others. In buying a skewed vision of power, many
women discount the importance of such qualities as nurturing, sensitivity, and perception, even as they understand how badly these are needed
in the running of not only the family but the world.

Expectation #6: From Now On I'll Only Do It My Way

Lying down and playing dead, going through life as a doormat, taking
care of everyone's needs but their own was the life script for so many
women for so long (and still is for so many others) that to suggest that

accommodation might be the answer at times is treading on dangerous ground. And yet, more and more frequently, I hear women say that they have learned to strike a balance between "settling" and reconciliation. Some say they have decided to go along with some of their husband's bad habits because "I really like the guy." Others admit that they are just plain tired of holding grudges against former lovers, old roommates, ex-husbands, or friends. A divorced woman of 40, after deciding to let go of the anger she'd felt about her husband for six years, told me recently that she felt as if she'd just lost "about fifty pounds of garbage" off her back. "I feel lighter, cleaner, and like I can breathe better. I realized that by holding on to that anger I was still allowing him to hold me back as he'd done for years."

Expectation # 7: If I Just Run a Little Faster, I'll Catch Up

Whether she's a rural housewife in the middle of Nebraska or the most motivated of businesswomen in the middle of Manhattan, the thought that lives with today's woman more than any other is: Everyone else is doing something more interesting than I am, and they are doing it better. They are happier/luckier/making more money/a better mother/prettier/thinner/younger/a better cook/further along in their career/sleeping with more interesting men/planning their lives better/taking more interesting trips. And after that thought, a second one always uncurls with the admonition: And if I just would run a little harder, I could catch up with the others. If I would just try a little harder, I could lose ten pounds/get my degree/get my husband to talk to me/get the promotion/get the kids all in school/get the perfect haircut/get him to fall in love with me/get rid of him/stop wasting so much time on the soaps/start reading more/stop going away every weekend/get organized/get the contract/get lucky. If I just try a little harder, run a little faster, I'll be there. But many women are finding that, as Gertrude Stein said in another context, "When you get there, there's no there there."

Expectation # 8: You Can Have it All

One of the most dangerous promises made by the decade is that as a woman you can now have it all. Not only should you be able to have a

promising career and marriage and children and a love life that will provide you with the plots for at least two romance novels, but you should
be able to have them all without ever being depressed, angry, tired, vulnerable, or guilty. Commenting on this expectation, my friend Eva described for me a poster of a woman burdened by a bulging briefcase in
one arm and the accoutrements of a household in the other, sighing
that she has "the worst of both possible worlds." Today the smorgasbord
of choices for women is tempting, but a wise woman knows she doesn't
have to sample everything to the point where she is fit only to waddle
away and take a nap.

The new expectations sound good when they are all lined up in
a row. They sound good because, on the face of it, they are good. A job
is often one of the things that makes life worth living: it provides money
and a form to your life, and sometimes it even provides travel and attention and an expense account and the feeling that you've made a difference in the world. Marriage and family can be fulfilling beyond belief and
the feel of a newborn baby against your skin or the sight of a child bring-
ing you breakfast in bed or graduating *magna cum laude* can break
your heart with happiness. Yes, there is almost nothing to equal the rush
you feel after you've really communicated on a deep level with another
human being.

However, since each of the new expectations is based on
doing—get a job, get married, talk more, try harder—they hold the risk
of providing further failure and pain unless you, the doer of them, connect with them on some level of your being. A job, no matter how attractive, can make you feel anxious or bored or totally exhausted unless it
has some meaning for you. A marriage, no matter how full it is of all the
right ingredients, can disintegrate into emptiness if the ingredients don't
make sense to you. And standing your own ground, no matter how admirable a concept, can sometimes leave you on a lonely island floating
out to sea, when all the time you just wanted to be sitting around on the
beach with the others.

Are there ways, then, for women to rethink the promise of choice and make it come true? Can we ignore the scenarios written by others, weigh the decade's expectations against our own, and at last feel secure enough to pick and choose from among life's options?

I believe that there are and that we can, and in the chapters that follow I have written of some of the ways some of us have allowed this to happen in our own lives.

2
Working Your Way to Oblivion

"Getting a Job Is the Answer"

About five years ago I'd been working on the near-edge of exhaustion as Women Helping Women moved from a regional to a national program. Teaching, counseling, writing course materials, getting ready for my son's high school graduation, battling a sore throat, I had come, this rainy night, to the end of four weeks' work on the presentation of a major grant proposal I'd written to extend the program. Government representatives and other mental health functionaries had been in and out of my office examining records, the cleverness and employability of my students, and me.

Now, at 8:00 P.M., as the rain turned to glare ice on the interstate,

I had just dropped the last visitor off at the airport in Minneapolis and sat, exhausted, over dinner. As I sat there in my tailored wool suit, my expense-account dinner before me, I watched the hostess of the restaurant. She was a woman about my age, but she looked relaxed and happy. I thought about her job. Why not? I've always loved wearing nice clothes. Dim light is becoming. I'm a gracious person who could certainly wave people to their tables easily enough, and how wonderful it would be not to bring my job home with me!

Later, in the restroom, I talked with the hostess. "How I envy you your work," I began, actually hoping to hear her say she needed a replacement a couple of nights a week. She stared at me in disbelief.

"You've got to be kidding. This is world-class pits. If I never see another person it'll be too soon!"

Then she told me that she only had three more months to go until she could quit. She had just finished a degree and was looking forward to a job in special education.

"But what I'd really like to do," she said as she walked out, "is just go home and sleep for about six months."

A few years before, when there was lots of talk about "shit-work"—that cleaning, wiping, and mopping up around the house which no one presumably wants to do and which is, therefore, left to the house-wife—I was at a meeting. I wanted very much to say to the leader that if we were going to prioritize distasteful tasks, I'd like to put grant writing right up there at the top of the list. But before I'd worked up the courage to say it, a woman on the other side of the room said that her idea of scutwork was being ready to leave work at five o'clock and having the boss pile a twelve-page report on her desk to be finished by morning.

We are all so beautifully human! We all want the job with the expense account, the ability to "make a difference," and decision-making power, and yet we want the hostess's dim lights. We want to feel as needed as the special-education teacher but, like the secretary, we want not to have to take our job home at night. Beyond everything, of course, we would all love just to go home and sleep for six months.

What we don't want is the constant need to create just to keep solvent, the 4:00 A.M. tossings and turnings and plannings, the daily battle with surly customers, dirty cocktail glasses, bosses who treat us like part of the furniture, cranky students who don't want to learn—or to have to wash the sheets on that bed we want to sleep in for six months.

What we want, of course, is everything.

For many women during the last twenty years, just getting a job seemed like having it all. For the woman who has to support her family, a job is a necessity. For the housewife, tired of staring at the four walls, the job seemed a possibility for rebirth. For the woman just out of college, a job is the place to put talent and training to work, and for the woman who comes from a family where no woman has ever worked outside the home before, it is a chance to model the new way. Money, freedom, self-esteem, and the chance to meet interesting people. Surely the happy ending was in sight.

But something has gone wrong. Increasingly, women are speaking up about the way they feel about their work:

- "If this is what I'm trained to do, why do I hate it so much?"

- "We decided I could stay home after the baby was born, but now my husband says we need the money, and besides all his friends' wives work."

- "I haven't read a book in years, and I can't remember the last time we had anyone over for dinner."

- "I'm exhausted half the time, and the rash is coming back between my fingers."

- "I'm thinking about quitting and having a baby."

- "Why doesn't my husband ever want to talk about *my* job?"

- "I dread getting in the car to go to work."

And underneath, largely unspoken but always manifest, are the bottom lines: "What's it all about, anyway?" and "Where did it all go wrong?"

Job as Answer

Where it all went wrong is when women began to buy the myth that a job is the answer. Not *an* answer, for a job can, indeed, be an answer to many of life's wants and needs; but *the* answer, the one way to live out one's life.

Just as marriage was once touted as the answer to everyone's dream of hapiness, so now has the job taken center stage as *the* way. To be a full-time homemaker is to feel not only vestigial but foolish in some circles, and not to want a briefcase and a blazer is to feel faintly obscene in others. Like marriage before it, which often broke under the strain of expectation, the opportunity for women to work at jobs outside the home stands in danger of becoming a flawed option because of the un-realistic expectations now being placed upon it. If jobs for women be-come the next casualty of expectation, we will have, to our peril, lost to the world of work the vital and creative power that women bring to it.

The notion of job-as-answer is a development of the last two decades and provides some clues to why women are finding that a job is often *not* the answer.

In decades past, women worked primarily because of economic or psychological need. It is only during the past few years that women have begun to get the message from the decade scenario writers that getting a job is the answer, whether to the problems in one's life, the emptiness of it, as a receptacle for one's talents, or to keep in step with everyone else.

Much as hysterectomies were once—and in some cases still are—urged upon women for a spectrum of "complaints," so now is the job often held out as the panacea for just about any problem a woman may have. This prescription is given out by a variety of people, among them doctors, ministers, counselors, the media, friends, and husbands.

"When one of these 'lost women' comes in to see me, I don't know what she's talking about half the time," a minister in Milwaukee told me as he puffed on his pipe. "What else is there to say except go back to school or get a job?"

But taking a job as an answer to a problem you haven't even defined makes about as much sense as taking medication for an undi-agnosed physical problem. Taking an entry-level job that you know will be routine is hardly an answer to feelings of worthlessness. Taking a job in your field that you despise so that "your talents won't go to waste" is a shortcut to waking up one morning and discovering you've wasted something far more precious: your life.

Because of the heavy expectations we have placed upon jobs for women, we ask of them far more than they can ever give. A job was, is, and always will be a piece of work for which you get paid. It can be exhilarating or challenging or it can be exhausting, stultifying, and boring. But what it can never be is *the* answer.

A colleague asked me recently why I persist in lumping professional and nonprofessional women together when I talk about job concerns. The answer is simple: The root of the problems and many of the manifestations of them are exactly the same. The concerns that women with families have about work do not fit neatly within age, geographic, economic, or educational categories. They crisscross and mesh to a degree that I could blindfold women from three different employment categories at the university where I work and within minutes have them discussing the same common concerns.

These are the two most prevalent concerns of wives and mothers who work outside of their home:

1. I never have enough time to get it all done/I'm exhausted all the time/I get no support from anyone.

2. This job is not fulfilling to me.

#1: "I'm Working Nine to Five—and Five to Nine"

Using a sample of 2,325 women between the ages of 25 and 65, University of Wisconsin economists Barbara Wolfe and Robert Haveman found that working mothers are not as healthy as working women who do not have children. They found that these women slept less, had less time to watch television, and read less than other women.

This comes as no surprise to Kayleen, a 30-year-old mother of four, who says, "I'm sick, sick, sick of having to come home from work at six and then start working all over again." She speaks for the thousands of women who not only work nine to five but then begin to work again at five when they pick up the groceries and continue on until nine and beyond as they bus meals, help kids with homework, and gather up dirty underwear and socks for the nightly laundry. "It's even worse than it was before when I was home all day bored out of my skull."

Marcie, a guidance counselor in an elementary school, taught before she was married, stayed home with her children when they were small, but then got her master's degree so that she could be a counselor. "I'm really committed to my work," she says, "but I am so far behind in everything I could scream. My kids will be gone before I know it, and I feel like we never spend any time together." She gives a self-conscious smile. "I'd give anything to stay home someday and just bake a pie."

Claudette is an attractive 60-year-old brunette who works as the personnel director for a large manufacturing company in St. Louis. As she orders her third drink, she apologizes to me.

"I know I drink too much. It's just that I'm so exhausted all the time it's the only way I ever calm down." Claudette gets severe migraines every few weeks, but she feels she can't afford to quit her job because she and her husband are putting in a pool this summer.

She continues: "When the kids left ten years ago I had this neat picture of Mike and me coming home from work each night, settling down over a drink, and talking about our day. Forget it. He says he's tired and just wants his dinner and some peace and quiet. 'I don't care if you work,' he says, 'but don't bring the damn job home.'"

For Kayleen, who has to work to support her family, for Marcie, who works because of a feeling of commitment, and for Claudette, who works because she both needs and wants to, the central problem is the same: there is never enough time or energy or support.

For the woman who works outside her home—as well as for all others—the operable word must be *reality*. The fewer games she plays with herself and others about the madhouse called her life, the freer and happier she will be. The first thing to remember is that no one is ever going to be as interested in what you are doing as you are. If you are interested in a clean house, getting to your karate lesson on time, getting the checkbook balanced or your Christmas presents bought, or a decision on what to serve your dinner guests on Friday, remember that the likelihood of anyone else's being interested is remote. Until it is Christmas, time for the dinner, or someone needs a clean shirt, it is unlikely that anyone but you is going to care about any of these things. Likewise, even though you are excited about how well your proposal for the new sales office in Des Moines went over with the boss, it is unlikely that your husband or children will have more than a passing interest in the fact.

If you are a listener and a "carer," you are at special risk if you are working both at home and on the job. The fact that *you* listen to and care about what others are doing, the fact that you care enough to pick just the right present for each relative or drive thirty miles out of your way to get violets for your dinner party, does not change this reality. It also does not necessarily mean that the other people do not care or that you are a carer and they are not.

Remember that people care about what they care about. You care about what you care about, and they care about what they care about. It is as simple—and as wildly nerve-racking—as that.

This does not mean that you cannot ask others for help or to listen to you or share with you. What it does mean is that you need always to cook, buy, learn, do, win for your own sake and enjoy it for its worth to *you*. If someone else can celebrate or grieve or get their hands dirty with you, wonderful. But be prepared for the fact that you may have to do it alone.

The Wet-Towel Reality Probe

In all the years I've directed Women Helping Women, I cannot remember a class, workshop, or television audience of women that has not brought up the apparently perennial, perhaps eternal question of how to get family members to pick up their dirty underwear and wet towels. As more and more women return to work outside their homes, this problem seems to surface even more frequently. It has become, in fact, a metaphor for the entire spectrum of household chores, and in the following discussion I will be using it that way:

The reality of wet towels and dirty underpants is that you have five choices:

1. You can successfully teach everyone to pick up her or his own things.

2. You can pick them up yourself.

3. You can hire someone to pick them up.

4. You can let them stay on the floor.

5. You can spend your life yelling at others to pick them up.

Women's first reaction to these choices is often "yes, but . . . " which is a waste of time since these are the realities of the situation. Instead, it is important for women to review the choices one by one and determine clearly what it would take to accomplish each one and what gains and losses would accrue from choosing one as opposed to another.

1. If you have a husband and/or children who are basically cooperative but mildly forgetful, it often works to mention that you'd like them to put the laundry in the hamper. I'm continually amazed at the number of women who have never asked anyone to help them, either assuming that (a) the other person(s) wouldn't or (b) the other person(s) should know it without being told. That kind of thinking, of course, only hurts one person—you.

If you are the mother of young children, it is important to know that kids don't suddenly turn into willing helpers at age ten. Unless you begin when they are three or four to ask for and expect their help, you are assured of running battles as they enter the teen years. When I began working for the news service when my youngest child was five, he and his two older sisters were already accustomed to making their own beds, picking up their toys, shoveling out their rooms once a week, and taking turns doing dishes, cleaning the playroom, and dumping trash. None of this happened because they were docile, overmotivated kids;

no one has ever described any one of them in those words! It happened because, from the start, I shared with them what had to be done and just how many of us there were to do it. They weren't docile, but they also weren't dumb, so when they saw the reality of the situation, they could handle it.

2.   Many women, as they confront the wet-towel problem, consider it easier simply to pick up the mess themselves. For one thing, it will be done the way they want it to be done. If having things done or disposed of properly is a priority with you, then do it, without apology, but understand that the time you take for that will have to be taken away from something else. Consider priorities: if this is a top one, then do it. If not, consider another option.

3.   There is absolutely nothing wrong with hiring household help, and yet the legacy of Suzy Homemaker dies hard for many women, and it seems somehow "lazy" to hire someone to clean up your family's mess. Even women who do finally employ help find themselves scurrying around at 6:00 A.M. to be sure the house is in order before the helper arrives. Other women think they cannot afford it. Ony after I had been hospitalized as a young mother from sheer exhaustion did we finally realize that we could afford the few dollars each week to hire someone to help with our nine-room house, even if it meant cutting things very, very close on a beginning teacher's salary.

4.   Many women are perfectly comfortable with letting dirty laundry lie on the floor. If you are one of those, by all means do it. If it bothers someone else, let that person tell you about it, and then you can negotiate with him or her. But be sure you are really comfortable with the mess on the floor. If you are letting it lie there to "show" someone or out of other manifestations of your anger, you are wasting your time and hurting yourself. The person you are trying to "show" will remain unimpressed: if he or she cared about whether it was on the floor, it would have long since been picked up or otherwise disposed of "properly." Your leaving it there as a lesson only perpetuates your own poisonous feelings and drains more of your limited energy.

5.   For the same reason, the choice of yelling about dirty laundry each day for the next twenty years is one to be made only if you have unlimited energy to devote to your frustration. An occasional scene over wet towels is all a part of family living, but a chronic battle on this subject suggests to me that a more productive release of tension might be to find a friend or counselor with whom to discuss your feelings.

Once you have made your decision about the wet towels, *go on to every other phase of running your household.* Consider meals— shopping, preparing, serving, clearing away. Consider cleaning itself, en- tertaining, gardening, the leaky faucet—the probe works in every in- stance. Just be sure to make decisions on how you will handle each based on reality, not upon wishes.

You may protest that it can't be done, but I have seldom seen a working woman whose schedule would not yield to the "reality probe." If you are willing to spend the time and the energy to make it happen, the results can be exciting.

#2: "I'm Not Doing Who I Am"

Writing from Oregon a couple of years ago, a woman described her own despair concerning her work as a nursing assistant: "My being and my employment are separate, and it's frustrating."

For many women, this separation of doing and being is a pain- ful reality they must face each time they get ready for work. For some of them it is because they feel stuck in entry-level jobs. For others, at the other end of the educational spectrum, the "stuckness" comes because they feel they have to "use" their college degrees or because they are moving up in careers they are not even sure they want. These women are caught in traps that I call the No-Talent Trap and the Talent Trap.

The No-Talent Trap: Jerry

"I feel bored and depressed when I go to work. I know I'm capable of doing something more fulfilling. I need to get out of this clerical job rut, but I don't know how."

The problem was clear. The client was Jerry, age 39, a high school graduate, married with two children, seven and ten. Her husband has a job but it is a seasonal one, so they need her income. She has been a typist at a medical clinic for the past eight years, taking only six months off when her second child was born. Jerry said she had "no talents" and expects to be doing the same thing for the rest of her life. The thought depresses her still further.

The suggestions I gave in working with Jerry in my office are the same ones I would give to other women caught in the No-Talent Trap:

1. Give yourself permission to think seriously about yourself.

2. Give yourself permission to think seriously about your job search.

Unless you take these seriously, you well may be trapped forever.

Begin at once to take yourself as seriously as you do your husband or your children. Set aside one complete day (take a vacation day from work or, if this is not possible, hire a sitter or ask your husband to watch the children on Sunday), take a notebook, pencil and your calendar, and go to a quiet place. If there is none in your home, go to the library.

Begin by listing your job priorities: money, autonomy, free time, vacations with your children, dressing the way you want to, career advancement. Consider what is really important to you, not what you think should be important to you. Be realistic. Even though we would all like the job that has it all, the reality is that every job has its drawbacks. Are you willing to spend six years on professional training, drive a hundred miles to the nearest big city, be a commuter wife? Or do you prefer the chance to work half days and have time for other things? Remember that "unfulfilling" jobs occur on all levels: there is no hierarchy of boredom. (Many women tell me, for example, that they would love to get into social work, but they often don't realize how exhausting it can be to deal with hurting people all day nor how tiresome and yes, boring, it can be to fill out the stacks of required forms.)

While you are at it, check out why you feel bored and unfulfilled at your present job. Is it the job or is it because you yourself feel empty? A job you enjoy can help, but don't ever expect a job to fill all the missing

places within you any more than you can expect a marriage or other relationship to do it.

List your skills. I have yet to meet a woman who has no skills or
no talents. Jerry, in addition to her typing skills, was a gourmet cook,
played the flute, could speak German, had a good soprano voice, had
taught Sunday school for five years, could do calligraphy, knit, and ice-
skate.

Next it is important to create or update your résumé. Get rid of
things that sound weak, add positive statements, jettison the erasures,
question marks, and et ceteras. For women who consider their lives to
be just one big et cetera, getting rid of the *etc*'s on their résumé forces
them into sharper thinking regarding their actual skills and goals. Add
the skills that you have identified in short, concise statements. In working
with Jerry, we upgraded her résumé by adding, under the category "ad-
ditional skills," the fact that she speaks German, plays the flute, and is
skilled in calligraphy. We also added the fact that she had been paid to
design and produce the invitations for the medical clinic's annual fund-
raising banquet each year under the "employment" category. We then
had the entire thing printed in offset type and placed in plastic binders.

The next step in this process is to look at your calendar and
block out one half hour each day that you will commit to thinking about
your job future. (Jerry at first said she couldn't find any time but finally
settled on the period from 9:00 to 9:30 each night after her children
were off to bed or homework and before the time she and her husband
usually watched television or talked together.) Use this time of the day to
think over the day, the progress you've made toward feeling better about
your life. Consider ways you can use your present job, no matter how
boring, to upgrade yourself: what have you learned about interpersonal
relations? about how your boss handles correspondence? time? people?
You might want to use a journal in which to write your feelings, perceptions, and goals.

As you begin to turn to your active search for a more fulfilling
job, remove the expresssion "justa" (as in "justa typist") forever from
your vocabulary and your mind. Remove also the belief that you have
"no talents." Since they are already down on a list, it is obvious that you
do have some.

At this point it is time to begin to set some realistic goals for
yourself. Realistic in this case means that they are *potentially* reachable

even though they will probably require time and hard work. Jerry decided that she would have the goal of a new job one year from the day we talked. She realized that she wanted one that dealt with people, had meaning for her, and had something to do with food, which was a love of hers.

Rather than simply circulating your résumé "over the transom" and doing a lot of hoping, it is important to plan ways to reach your goal. Go to the library and look at recent books on careers. Instead of using a prepared book list, it can be helpful to seek out your own books; the search itself is a valuable lesson. Some women will want to go to a career counseling center at a nearby university or women's center and watch the newspaper for job seminars in their area. Jerry chose to read *What Color Is Your Parachute?* by Richard Bolles, attend a course in food-service management at a vocational school, and take a two-session financial planning seminar at a local bank.

Women who have not interviewed for a job lately need to find an up-to-date book on interview procedures and read it, attend a course in which interviewing techniques are practiced, or talk with a career counselor. Many otherwise qualified women lose jobs at the interview because they concentrate on what they can't do ("I'm not familiar with engineering terms") instead of what they can do or can learn to do. Jerry, because of working with the public all day in her job at the clinic, felt she presented herself well and did not need further practice in this area. I agreed.

Without making a public announcement that would jeopardize your existing job, the next step is to begin to find out what else might be available to you. Consider the possibility of upgrading yourself within your own company. Check with trusted friends who will keep your search quiet until the appropriate time to announce it. Check out people in the field in which you are interested. Decide upon a fair date on which you will give notice to your present employer.

Remind yourself each week of your goal date for the new job, and take it seriously. As long as you consider a job upgrade to be a "sometime" thing, it will remain just that—maybe even for the rest of your life. Jerry's first appointment with me was in November. She did her goal setting and résumé writing in December and January, read the book in January, took the food-service course from January to May, took the financial seminar two nights in February, and began making job inquiries in March. She talked with people in the food service at the clinic where she worked but decided that a job there would not bring any more fulfillment than her present job.

At this point I suggested she design a "dream job." In this process, you let your imagination create the job you would really like to have, given your existing skills and talents, if you could create it. Jerry said she would like to be a singer in a supper club, laughing at herself as she said it.

In April Jerry began her serious job search by talking with owners of three restaurants. In May she found the job that, as a typist, she would have never allowed herself to dream of: a woman who had just opened a restaurant near a university campus hired Jerry to work as dining room manager five days a week and to calligraph the menus and signs. The salary was more than half again as much as Jerry had been earning. Two months after Jerry began working she got a bonus she would never have received had she not redone her résumé: she was asked to play her flute during the lunch hour two days each week! The dream of being a performer in a club was not as unrealistic as Jerry had believed it to be.

Jerry's story is typical of most women caught in the No-Talent Trap. The success with which a woman is able to get out of her routine job and move on to a more fulfilling job depends almost entirely on her willingness to take herself and her job search seriously.

The Talent Trap: Susan

"I feel so guilty."

Susan is 28, married, very attractive, and the graduate of a small private college in the East. The first year of her marriage she had worked as a cocktail waitress. She liked the job very much because it gave her a chance to work with people and allowed her time to study, paint, and cross-country-ski. But Susan had also majored in art education, and so she quit the waitress job and took one as an art teacher in a private school.

"I loved my student teaching," she recalls, "but I found I just couldn't stand the 'dailiness' of dealing with the kids week after week. I started getting migraines and spending every weekend just sleeping to make up for the rest of the week. So I quit at the end of the first year." Now she is feeling guilty for not "using" her education.

Over lunch with Susan we evaluated her situation. On the surface it looked to be ideal. Her husband was earning a good living as a gynecologist, and he wanted to leave the decision as to whether she went back to work up to her.

I asked her about her life. What parts had she really enjoyed?

"I'm embarrassed to say this, but I was really happy when I was working at the lounge." I asked her to list what she had liked about that job. She said that it had allowed her to be with interesting people (most of them had been students, writers, or artists just starting their work) and that the job, an evening one, had allowed her the chance to sleep late in the morning. She liked the fact that she didn't have to bring the job home and that it allowed her free time to read, write, paint, or "just goof around", which she admitted she loved to do. What hadn't she liked about the job? She never got to see her husband except on weekends, her mind was getting "stagnant," and . . .

"And what?"

"I feel so guilty."

The guilt that Susan felt and which so many other women express to me is that "I *should* be using my education."

Guilt came up again in Houston, where I'd gone to do a consultation. I was met at the airport by a woman in her early thirties who soon confided to me how guilty she felt for not using her M.B.A. even though she loved her job as administrative assistant to the man I had come to work with.

The nagging persistence of the educational "should" can become a kind of water torture if we let it; a degree will provide us freedom of choice only if we allow it. Women who are beset with this particular form of guilt need to remind themselves that most professional skills are translatable into other job families; no training need be wasted. If you trained as a musician, can you honestly say the years of your training were wasted even though you are not "doing something" with your degree? And how does the "doing something" translate for you? As Richard Frisbie wrote about women years ago in *How to Peel a Sour Grape: An Impractical Guide to Successful Failure:*

One reason [women] are dispirited is that they are victims of the
same utilitarian outlook as men. They feel apologetic about
anything they do that doesn't earn money. Making ceramics in a
basement kiln is only amateur dabbling, but selling someone
else's ceramics part-time in the neighborhood gift shop is a
worthwhile job, and writing ads full-time for someone else's
ceramics for the department store downtown is a career. . . .

In working with Susan I asked her, as I had Jerry, to "dream," but
since her focus was not on getting a job, I asked her to dream about her
life. What would it be like if she could design it?

Susan's priorities were to have time for her marriage and have
weekends free to enjoy skiing, sailing, and golf with her husband, to get
out with her own friends as well as those in their circle of married friends,
to work at a job she didn't have to bring home, go to graduate school
(for interest purposes only at this time) and do something that would
involve children.

I talked with Susan a year ago. Today she is working in the print
restoration division of an art museum three afternoons a week, and on
the remaining two days she conducts tours for elementary children who
visit from the city schools. This gives her the mornings to sleep, paint,
and "goof around." She has been accepted into the master's program in
art history and attends classes one morning and two evenings a week.
One or two evenings a week she goes out with friends. Her weekends
are free to spend with her husband. Her migraines are gone, and she
feels good about her life.

She admits that the old guilt feelings still hit her once in a while,
especially when she is at a party with her husband surrounded by, as she
says, "the fast-track crowd," and someone asks her what she "does."

"More and more," she said, "I've learned to look them directly in
the eye and tell them, without hesitation or apology. The strange thing is,
most of them say it sounds really good. They almost sound envious."

For women in their late thirties, forties, and fifties who have
worked twenty-four-hour days for a decade or more to make it in a career or to create something they wanted to see happen, talent and training can sometimes feel like twin sandbags they must never put down.

One such woman told me she would like to retire but was afraid that "with the job gone there might be no one there."

Recently Meg, a minister friend of mine, described a typical career pattern we've both seen among women who are now in their forties, fifties, and sixties. Starting out as a full-time wife and mother, these women went on to get degrees at a time when that was not the accepted thing to do. They were often alone and lonely, but they kept at it. When they finished their training they took, with great joy, the first job available to them. In this job, because they were often the "first" or the "only," they had to "chop wood and haul water." Finally, after "busting their butts" and proving themselves through years of hard work, they were offered the Big Chance. But by then they were too tired to take it.

Several years ago a student of mine told me about such a woman, a friend of hers, who had worked hard as an architect to get to the top of her profession and then became exhausted by the never-ending demands on her time. Her assistant was new to the field and eager to move ahead. This wise and creative woman, trusting her assistant's abilities and her own instincts, simply exchanged jobs with her, allowing each of them what they most needed at that time in their lives.

Not many of us have the luxury of these ideal circumstances, but many of us as professionals have many more options for choice than we may imagine. As my colleague Sue Taft, director of counseling at Thomas More College, has said so simply yet so wisely: "A job should not break our bones or our spirit." Here again each woman must take the time to find her own answers.

For Susan, this was the time to forget about teaching. On the other hand, maybe the woman on the fast track in Boston does not really want the boutique so much as she wants fewer obligations on weekends or a longer time in Maine next summer. As for Meg's comments about women being too tired to enjoy the "big finish," perhaps it is just another way we can be reminded that the happy ending had better be lived along the way, even as we are "busting our butts."

Once, dragging myself back from a particularly long and tiring trip, I found on my office door a poster put there by my teenage daughter. Two mountain climbers congratulated themselves, one at the peak of the mountain and one almost there. But on the other side, out of sight of the climbers, the mountain showed itself to be an unfriendly monster with arms folded in impatience.

"Success," it read, "is never what it seems."

Perhaps it is time for all of us to rethink our individual perceptions of success. Perhaps it is time to consider the words of David Maitland in his book *Against the Grain: Coming through Mid-Life Crises,* in which he speaks of the "deprivations for which no income will compensate."

Of course I did not take the hostess job. But I have, of necessity and the desire to stay alive, designed some of my own retreat strategies, which allow me to back off from the exhaustion intrinsic in my work. Sometimes I escape for a couple of days to a good hotel where I can enjoy breakfast in bed and a sauna. Other times my retreat is a walk along the river behind my house or the purposeful letting go of a chance for another "success" in exchange for more free time. Other times I do bake that bread or simply hold my cat in my lap and stare at the fire or spend an entire day doing absolutely nothing.

I think it is important for women to remember, in this time when board meetings appear to have replaced bake sales, that the worth of what we do is not in the eye of the beholder. What you consider meaningless, I may wish to have time to do. And what you consider boring at one time in your life may be just what you want and need to do at another. As long as it is an honest choice rather than a dishonest copout, as long as you realize the consequences, it is probably right for you at this time.

The lives we lead as women and what we fill them with, the work we do or don't do, can only be defined by us. There is nothing magical about working outside the house any more than there is something intrinsically sacred about working only within it. We are the only ones who can put the magic and sacrament wherever we are.

But first we have to believe it ourselves.

3

The Invisible Housewife

"Staying Home Is the Answer"

A woman sits in my office and tells her story: "I graduated from high school in 1970 and got married the next year. My first child was born a year later and my second one three years after that. As the marriage went on I lost all the self-confidence I had as a young girl and I eventually lost myself. I was a mother, wife, cook, lover—and failure. When I turned thirty I realized that this was it. This was my life. The guy on the white horse had already been here. If I wanted anything better, I was going to have to help myself to it. I had had it with failure. I was going to do something about my life."

Failure did not appear to be something that the brunette at the hairdresser's had felt often in her life. She had smoky dark hair swept off a creamy complexion. She was a flight attendant based in Minneapolis. She was having her nails done, and she was going to be 30 years old the next day. "Choices are the big problem for women today," she said. "Now that I'm thirty, I'm really struggling with them. When I think of my career, the value of it and what the payoff will be at the end, it seems small compared with what the payoff would be for having children and raising a family."

In those two stories, one of failure turned to promise and the other of promise turned to doubt, is the continuing paradox of marriage and family.

Marriage *is* an incredible paradox, and a marriage with children in it even more so. It can provide our most joyous times and our most deadly. The very person we most love can become the trigger for our deepest despair; the children to whom we gave life can seem, at times, to drain ours away from us. As one woman wrote, in referring to her marriage, "The things that I wanted all my life became the things which ended up making me unhappy."

Any woman who has ever managed a home and family is fully aware that it is a job without pay which requires, as one of my students wrote, that we provide the skills of "money management, house maintenance, social director, nurse, intermediary, transportation expert, decorator, cultural expert, psychologist, and family-relations and child-development specialist. We deal," she concluded, "with the reality of maintaining life."

And yet the thought of a life without marriage can make many women feel bereft. For others, the thought that they may never bear a child is a devastating one that haunts the wee hours of their lives. More and more as I travel I talk with 30- and 40-year-old women who are pregnant, thinking of becoming pregnant, or sorry that they aren't pregnant. It seems only the day before yesterday that women were asking who needed motherhood, only the day after that women talked with me about how they could juggle jobs and babies, and now, increasingly, women mention quitting their jobs entirely to devote full time to child rearing.

It all sounds so good, this "baking bread and writing poems," as one woman called it. After years of punching time clocks, battling morning traffic, and eating fast food every night, the thought of setting one's own schedule has tremendous appeal. It sounds to many, in fact, as if it just might be the answer.

When I began my counseling practice in 1971, funeral preparations were under way for the institution called marriage. Bent, nearly broken, under the weight of too many expectations, marriage had come to be regarded as a hopelessly outdated ceremony that prevented rather than enhanced the full expression of an individual's life. I have participated in the writing and celebrating of many "alternative" marriage ceremonies, ceremonies done in parks and woodlots and apartments with lots of daisies and white wine and lots of hopes that by avoiding the constricting language of their parents' ceremonies the newlyweds could avoid the constricted lives their elders had seemed to live.

In violent and often well-founded reaction to what had gone before, women very purposefully began to prepare for careers. It suddenly became not only all right for a girl to be valedictorian instead of prom queen but better.

It was this concept of "better" again, this ranking of what was "good" and what was not, that triggered the reaction that has followed. Once confined to the doll corner in kindergarten, little girls found that their playrooms could not be considered complete without a dump truck or two; daddies found that daughters were not worth bragging points anymore if they weren't in medical school or, at the very least, studying accounting. The girls who still genuinely liked being on the pom-pom squad were looked upon with disdain, and women who sincerely wanted to teach or to be nurses were accused of falling into the "nurturing trap."

One of today's best kept secrets is that there are still millions of housewives out there.

Praised by her community as the one to count on when things get rough, told she isn't using her potential (yet often wondering if she has any), still counted on heavily by her husband and children to keep things running smoothly in the family, the housewife now has to face up to the fact that, according to media reports, she no longer exists.

Even worse, there will be no benefit dance on her behalf because, if there were, she would have to be the one to organize it, and right now she's too tired.

The word "housewife" translates benignly enough as "a married woman who manages a household," but over the past decade the word has taken on a connotation that makes us want to hold it at arm's length much as we would the piles of dirty laundry it has come to represent. Angered by memories of the stagnation of our early lives—or those of our mothers—we have attempted to destroy a word that cannot easily be replaced. Attempts at euphemization—"homemaker," "household engineer"—have never become established in the vernacular because it was never the word but what the word came to mean that we have wanted to destroy.

In our attempt to jettison the concept of the mindless, ever-smiling scrublady, we have also jettisoned the word that describes the creative, powerful, exhausting, and lonely work being done by millions of women. As a result, housewives are left with the game but not the name, pitied at best and ignored to the point of invisibility at worst.

In one of history's most widely reported yet least authentic pendulum swings, women were reported to be leaving their homes in droves, not only physically (which they have) but emotionally, to enter the promised land of the paying job. The fact that many of them have not left emotionally brought the pendulum swinging back, until now, after a period of decline, marriage has retaken its place as a preferred life alternative.

Once again, it is not only all right but expected that a woman can talk about alençon lace and the relative merits of tea length versus cathedral length.

And once again, the dangerous myth of happily ever after settles itself square in the middle of the two-bedroom townhouse and dares the occupants to challenge it.

Princes into Frogs

When a woman and a man stand up to exchange wedding vows, they do not stand alone. Surrounding them is a cloud of expectations—some stated, some only hoped for, and others not yet realized or articulated—but all converging in the dream of a happy ending.

At this time and in this place, as at no other, are gathered the hopes of all the years. Except for the bride and bridegroom, everyone senses this and makes peace with it, each in his or her own way—some by tears, some by busyness, some with champagne, and some with prayer. For the woman and the man there is a sort of providential twenty-four-hour anesthesia that mercifully prevents them from realizing that an army of expectations walks behind them in the recessional. Only later must they "come to" and deal with them.

Much has changed in the fifteen years since I began my counseling practice, but the two major expectations couples have of marriage have remained startlingly static to this day.

The *first expectation* is that marriage per se will provide the happy ending.

Over much of time women have, of necessity, considered marriage to be a goal in life, an event that provided them with release from something they thought to be worse, such as loneliness, and that conferred upon them worth by reason of being chosen. Incredible as it may seem, given the events of a decade in which the road to divorce was paved with marriage's broken dreams, vestiges of this belief remain to this day.

A little pamphlet describing a wife was published by *Good Housekeeping* magazine in 1957. It stated that "a girl becomes a wife with her eyes wide open." Many of those "girls" may have had their eyes open, but what they were seeing was not the reality of marriage and family but the fantasy. Seldom, even today, is much thought given to what happens during that time which in fairy tales is called living happily ever after—a time never described because the authors knew that it is too complicated (or conflicted or boring) to attempt.

Here are the stories of some of the women who believed that marriage would provide their happy ending:

- "I was married after my senior year in high school. I was so in love and yet so naive about life and its responsibilities. Now I find myself unskilled, depressed, and without confidence. Sometimes I feel my greatest accomplishment is just to make it through the day." (Age 23)

- "I was 19 when I got married; the world was my oyster. I stayed 19 for 25 years. Now I'm 21. (Age 45)

- "Before I got married I lived on my own for ten years. I had a good job. I really liked it. But I got tired of hassling roommates and hassling my family about why I wasn't married. I thought it might be neat to try it, but now I feel like an unpaid maid. If he was starving he couldn't make a sandwich for himself." (Age 34)

- "I'm 56—young at heart but feeling old and useless. My husband is wonderful, but. . . . We have four wonderful children and two grandchildren, but. . . . Where do I go from here?

- "I was the marketing director for a publishing house. Every week I made decisions involving thousands of dollars. Now I'm home with my first baby, and some days I can't decide whether to put him in the yellow outfit or the red. What's happening to me?" (Age 37)

- "I turned 23 last week, which makes me one of 'today's women,' but I feel like I'm 40. I've got the same problems my mom had. This is progress?"

What is it about marriage that turns these talented, caring, decisive women into frightened, depressed, angry wives and mothers? How did their dreams of happiness go so severely awry that, as one woman put it, "From the moment I said my wedding vows it has been downhill all the way"?

The expectation that the marriage itself is going to be the happy ending, without any work on the part of the participants, carries in it the seeds of disaster.

From this belief in the perfection of marriage itself grows its corollary: you make *things* (in this case, marriage) more perfect by sacrificing *people* (you and your husband). Should I live to be one hundred, I would never have time to recount all the stories I've heard from women who have sacrificed themselves, their talents, and their interests on the altar of marriage, only to have the marriage die along with their sacrifices.

Sometimes sacrifices are made at the insistence of others: don't go to work/go back to work/get pregnant; but more often they are made because we ourselves think that they are demanded of us.

Since it is so easy to get love mixed up with sacrifice, we can find ourselves slipping into sacrificial patterns almost before we become aware of it. We go to sleep one day feeling strong and worthwhile; we awake to find that we are "nothing but a big vacuum cleaner" or that all the days are the same or that we cannot even remember the color of our own eyes.

As strong and free as I felt as a new wife, I succumbed by my late twenties to the notion that by denying my own needs I would be a better wife and mother. Not only did I do the expected thing and give up my work, but I also gave up all of the other things I'd loved—the dancing, the theater, the reading, the library browses, and the pub crawls—because they were "not what a mother does."

"What a mother does" is different in each decade, but the commitment to doing whatever "it" is remains firmly entrenched in our collective belief systems. Because of what "it" used to be, sacrifice very often became omission. Now, because "what a mother does" is often work on the job and at home until she is numb with exhaustion, self-sacrifice can also be defined as overextension.

"The Gift of the Magi," O. Henry's short story in which a husband and wife sacrifice prized possessions for each other's happiness, has become a staple in marriage and family classes as a testimony to the horrors that can occur when communication breaks down in a marriage. On the contrary, I not only find the story to be perennially refreshing, but also use it to demonstrate how sacrifice can be used within a marriage to enhance it.

The story, in which the wife has her long hair bobbed to earn enough money to surprise her husband with a fob for his prized pocket watch, just as her husband is off selling the watch to buy combs for her hair, points out the difference between negative and positive sacrificing within marriage. In sacrificing *things* for each other, the couple demonstrated the love on which the relationship was based and without which no marriage can survive with meaning. This is quite different from the dangerous sacrifice of individuals—their hopes, their dreams, their very beings—which brings so many marriages to the edge of disaster and beyond.

But even in sacrificing on behalf of people, particularly if those people are children, the sacrifice can backfire. Sacrificing on behalf of, doing for and giving to others is only loving and strengthening to them and to ourselves if it is well-considered and authentic.

One of my most vivid memories of my early days of counseling couples was a young wife and mother of five who came to my office just before Christmas in a state of near-exhaustion. Not only was she battling the depression and shaky marriage on which we had been working, but now she had spent the entire morning baking pans, jars, trays, and cupboards full of Christmas cookies. When I asked her what had made her decide to do all this, given her chronic tiredness, she said she "had to" because her husband expected it of her.

"Did he say so?" I asked.

"No," she answered, "but his mother always bakes tons of cookies at Christmas."

That evening I had an appointment with her husband. As he walked into my office he threw himself down on a chair.

"Whew, it's good to get away from that damn smell."

"What smell?"

"Cookies! The house reeks of them. I didn't like the things when my mom made them, and now Lynn's doing the same thing."

While most of us can see that there was a lot more going on here than cookies and that this episode is exemplary of many conflict points in the relationship, I mention it to show what happens to us when we "do" for others out of an assumption that they want it done. When we wonder why our husband doesn't jump for joy over the new velour smoking jacket we've surprised him with or why our kids don't smother us with kisses for serving them a nutritionally significant meal each evening, we need to remember that when we do for others because we think we should or because it is something we wish others would do for *us,* the results can be problematical. Once in a while you may find that you've hit the mark. More often than not you will never really know.

This does not mean that you quit giving to or doing for others. But you need to give and to do only after a careful evaluation of the recipient's actual needs and your actual capacity to give. *You must give only what you can psychologically afford to give, knowing there may be no thanks or reward.* Grudging gifts sour relationships; doing things because you have to sours lives. Children need mothers in their lives, not martyrs.

If a marriage relationship demands things that you cannot honestly give, it needs to be discussed and reevaluated. Perhaps the relationship will end. That is the chance you have to take. At least it is an honest statement of reality rather than a dishonest living out of a life.

Giving does not magically become easier once you are inside a marriage or have your arms around a child. That only happens if the reason you are in that marriage or have that child is because that is what you have honestly chosen and because you care so much for that marriage or that child that giving is what you want to do.

I recall with horror the number of times I have asked students in my marriage and family classes how many of them thought their parents had a happy marriage and not a hand has gone up! When I pressed for reasons in the discussion that followed, some of the students spoke of marriages that were conflicted, but most of them spoke of marriages about which they wondered why their parents had gotten married in the first place.

I've always believed that there are some things in life that no one should enter into unless the call to do so is so strong that it cannot be resisted. Among these are dark caves, the ministry, and marriage. I doubt that I would be married today if I hadn't felt that call.

Although it was the 1950s and although I had entered with some degree of enthusiasm into two previous engagements and assorted friendships, it was not until I met the man who is now my husband that the whole notion of marriage made any sense to me at all. Better, I had felt, to earn my own living and have my own fun than to be tied down to one person. But here, suddenly, was this person with whom I knew I wanted to make a public long-term commitment because there was no way I could not do it.

The shocked bewilderment with which my family and friends greeted this news notwithstanding, I married this man because I had to—not the hurried "had-to" so common in the fifties, but the had-to that seems to me to be the only reason anyone would want to enter into this most strange of institutions.

My had-to was not based on romantic flights of moonlit fantasy, although there was that, too. Neither was it based on endless considerations of our suitability for each other. We got married, in fact, two months after our first meeting. But in that time of getting acquainted, we had the chance to assess each other's honesty, dependability, capability for having fun, sex appeal, financial status, food and movie preferences (on which we've never been in agreement), family background, and potential for parenthood. How long, after all, does one need to assess these things?

It has been said repeatedly, yet somehow the truth of the words remains elusive: marriage requires the participation of two mature human beings each of whom could—if push came to shove—manage on their own. Anyone who cannot bear to be alone some of the time, manage money, make themselves a meal, take the car to be repaired, or understand that everyone needs respect and freedom has no business entering into a marriage.

Marriage never has been and never will be the place to escape for economic security, a sexual fix, or a good meal. There are so many other places that provide those things just as well at far less psychic cost. Marriage is, instead, the public celebration of what *is* in a relationship and of what that relationship can become. Marriages can grow and they can falter, but they cannot make something better that was not good when it began.

My own marriage has had times of intense pain, loneliness, and conflict as well as all of the fun that it promised to have in that first Wyoming spring. But never, ever, no matter how good or how bad things have become, have I ever wondered why the marriage took place.

Unless that answer is clearly apparent the day of a wedding, the crazy relationship called marriage doesn't stand much of a chance.

Brief Interlude with Baby

On a recent trip east I sat at dinner with three couples in their thirties. Two of the women had first babies under six months of age and had cut back their jobs to half time until that six-month mark. The third woman was pregnant.

The women told of their hectic lives. One told of trying to conduct an early-morning meeting while "bursting" with milk. Both mothers spoke of never having time to be with their husbands in the evenings because of erratic schedules of meals, baby care, and work brought home.

"We realized this would be a hard time," one of the women said, motioning toward her husband, an attorney. "But it's worth the sacrifice now because we know it will ease up in a year or so." She sighed when she mentioned how good it would be to read a book all the way through again and to get caught up on correspondence.

This picture of child rearing as a brief interlude that begins with the first labor pain and ends with the child's first spoonful of puréed tofu is one that has been held up over the past few years to working women as the way motherhood can be handled. It contrasts sharply with most women's reality, as described by this 27-year-old mother of an 18-month-old:

"I'm up at six each morning to start breakfast, get the baby up, feed her, call my husband, lay out his clothes. For the next twenty-three hours I take care of the baby. By mid-morning I have the beds made, the house picked up, and a couple of loads of laundry done. Where does all this laundry come from? By then the baby has probably walked into the cat's dinner or something else that needs cleaning up. If I'm lucky I get my teeth brushed by noon, and then it's time to fix lunch and start all over again.

"This doesn't even mention her bath, playing with her, taking her for a walk if the weather's halfway decent. This is heaven: the other day I thought I'd died and gone there when I got to take her out and pull her in the wagon. First time I've been anywhere in the daylight in over a month. Next comes what passes for her nap, but she hardly ever sleeps anymore. If she does, I always think I'm going to use the time to read or do something 'significant,' but I'm usually so tired I just watch soaps and fall asleep. Then it's time to thaw something for dinner, and then dishes and then read to her and get her ready for bed, and by nine o'clock I'm a zombie. Crawling into bed and turning the electric blanket up to 10 is the highlight of my day. At least I can get some rest."

Mothers of small children find themselves somewhere along the continuum between these two stories, but most of them cluster closer to the second story, even if they have household help or use day-care centers.

Seldom acknowledged at initial announcements of pregnancy or at baby showers is the fact that a baby is an eighteen-year commitment that involves, even with assistance from others, large chunks of your time and thought. The reality is that if you take time out to be with your baby, you will lose some of your career momentum. The other part of that reality is that if you don't take time out to be with your baby, you will lose the opportunity to have input into her or his development.

The reality is that, with babies, the "arsenic hour" comes now for my friend, Ardith, who had her babies after reaching the top of her profession, just as surely as it came for me twenty-five years ago when I was home with three children under four and had not even thought about returning to mine.

Women with young children have been written about so frequently that I continue to be surprised when one of them fails to realize that contact with an adult other than her husband is not a luxury but a necessity for the maintenance of mental health.

I should not really be surprised, I suppose, for I remember how my own arguments went on this subject when I was home full time with my own three children: I'm an intelligent woman. I don't need someone else to entertain me. I really don't have anything to say or know anyone I particularly want to say it to. I'm too tired and, besides, we can't afford a sitter. Having said all this, I would then greet my husband at the door with a dayful of complaints, expecting from him not only comfort and answers but entertainment to make up for the drabness of my own day. When these were not always forthcoming, I accused him of being uncaring and uncommunicative. It was only after I had gone back to a job outside the house that I realized how he must have felt as he walked through that door each night.

If you are at home with young children and can afford a regular helper, by all means hire one. If not, you must negotiate child-care trade-off with your husband or schedule a baby-sitter or other child-care for a minimum of one afternoon and one night a week, *no exceptions.* (If you were my client, this would be a requirement for continuing on in counseling with me!) The afternoon provides you with the chance to go swimming, take a class, visit a friend, go to the library, sit in your room and read, write, cry, or take a nap. The evening provides you time to go out. Once in a while the going out must be for some fun with your husband, or you will almost assure yourself that when your children have left home you will look at each other and wonder what you are still doing together. Baby-sitters or other child care must be one of the last items in your budget to be cut out, and then only if you are quite literally starving. It is *absolutely vital* to your physical and mental health and to that of your family. Hundreds of women over the years have told me they could not afford child care, but in each case we have worked out ways that they did. It is a matter of prioritization based on reality.

Mothers of young children also need to be very intentional about establishing a support system for themselves made up of at least one but preferably three or four friends. These should be people who are upbeat at least some of the time: problems squared are not only disastrous but measurably debilitating. These friends should also be people whom you feel free to phone and visit when you want or need to see them. Take this need seriously and ignore comments from those who regard phone calls to friends as frivolity or who think that because you have a job or don't have a job, you don't need help.

Once More without Feeling

The belief that things will get better by themselves is also at the heart of the second expectation of marriage: that it has the power to correct what was wrong in the relationship before the marriage. In-laws, money, overactive libidos, and underactive checkbooks are all, according to this expectation, to be transformed into workable entities by that great magician known as marriage. Recently I overheard a discussion in a restaurant on how the nagging question of who would give up whose career for whom to move where would be solved once the vows had been spoken.

There are two different ways in which marriage is said to be able to make these modifications and corrections:

The first is the old notion that whatever the problem, the marriage will heal it. Edith, 62, has lived her life on the basis of this belief. Although her husband was undemonstrative and unemotional for the year they were engaged, she had high hopes that once they were married he would start doing and saying the things she wanted to hear, such as "I love you." When he didn't, she began first to wonder, then to nag, and then to sulk. Now, almost forty years later, she is considering divorce because she is tired of his ignoring her feelings.

"He always says I'm making too much of things," she said. "He may be hurting, too, but instead of sharing the hurt with me he just keeps it to himself and then makes fun of me when *I* hurt. I just want him to let me know he loves me. When I ask him he always says, 'I'll let you know when you're not okay.'"

I worked with Edith using the Wet-Towel Reality Probe because the same five clear choices are available to Edith:

1. Get him to change his ways by something you say or do that convinces him he wants to reciprocate. (Ask others to pick up the towels.)

2. Get satisfaction and feelings of appreciation and self-worth from other areas such as friends or personal accomplishments. (Pick them up yourself.)

3. Go for marriage counseling. (Hire someone to pick them up.)

4. Let the situation stay exactly as it is. (Leave them on the floor.)

5. Spend the rest of your life wishing the situation were different, meanwhile nagging at him to change. (Yell at people to pick up the towels.)

The final choice, of course, is for her to go through with the divorce. (Throw the towels away.) The one choice that is not now, never was, and never will be available to her is to let the marriage itself solve the problem. (Expect the towels to leap off the floor themselves and re-align themselves on the rack.)

The second way that marriage is expected to be able to make a relationship better is the much newer and seemingly more intelligent method called the fifty-fifty marriage.

High hopes have been held out for the fifty-fifty marriage, in which lists of duties and responsibilities are contracted for before or early in the marriage. Most of us who have taught marriage and family classes since 1970 have discussed this with our students, but somehow this idea has never really worked. What went wrong?

Contracts are meaningless unless they are "keepable." What happens, then, when you have an opportunity to do a workshop at a sales conference in San Francisco on the week you have contracted to buy groceries and cook meals? Do you leave your children to go without eating or does your husband take over, thereby (in the literal sense) breaking the contract? What about his total inability to clean the refrigerator or toilet to your satisfaction even though he carries out these duties to the letter of the law? Do you redo the work (and break the contract), give thanks that you have a husband who will touch a toilet brush, seethe about it for the next quarter-century, or make it part of the grounds for divorce?

What happens when someone has had the kind of day that demands a back rub and it's the other person's turn to have some "space" that evening? What happens when you get a call from school that your daughter has been taken to the hospital after falling from the parallel bars in gym just as you are starting to assist your boss with a root canal and it's your week to tote and fetch the kids? On and on it goes, becoming more impossible as the marriage unfolds.

Recently, within a period of a week, I participated in three events surrounding the subject of ironing that provide a sort of intergenerational comment on the folly of *a priori* task assignment:

A couple in their sixties mentioned over dinner that a friend of theirs had just remarried. The newlywed husband had expected his new wife to do the cooking, cleaning, and ironing just as his first wife had, but wife number two refused, saying that ironing was not only outdated but redundant. "What kind of wife," my dinner companions asked, "is she?"

A few days later, at a large cast party, a young woman from the university came up to tell me about a problem that she was having with her boyfriend.

"We're going to get married in the spring and we've been trying to work up this list of who'll do what. I want him to take care of the ironing but he won't, and it really bugs me. After all, I'm going to do the damn cooking."

These recitals of unreal expectation occurred just after a business trip on which I'd worn a camel suit and a red blouse that my husband had ironed for me the night before I left because (1) I didn't have
time and (2) he is by far the better ironer.

Our own response to the myth of the fifty-fifty marriage has
been to meet one another's needs in ways that are lovingly pragmatic.
Just as the sight of a person stumbling under a load of bundles while
trying to maneuver a revolving door does not call for a "sex check" to
see who does what, neither (do we believe) does the spectacle of a wife
or husband rushing to make a deadline call for gender role entrench-
ment on the part of the other partner.

For us, fifty-fifty has meant that if one of us sees that something
needs doing, we do it. If something needs doing that one of us can do
better than the other, it is pretty obvious who should be doing it. This has
translated out, in our particular marriage, to his doing the car and electri-
cal repair (he's a mechanical genius), ironing (he worked as a presser
while in college), yard work (more muscle), and running the sewing ma-
chine to repair kids' clothes (back to mechanical genius). My tasks have
included cleaning and laundry (which I admit I've always enjoyed), writing everything from Christmas cards to letters to both our master's papers (I'm the better writer), and planning everything that needs to be
planned (he often can't find his calendar). Cooking, shopping, and child
care have been shared. We have never spent much time figuring any of
this out; life has always seemed much too short and far too filled with
other things to waste time discussing who is going to take out the
garbage.

There was much talk, during the years when marriage did its
fade-out, about what a legalistic sham it is. More recently in attempts to
"free it up," couples have, in fact, made it even more legalistic, by the use
of task and performance contracts, subcontracts and subsub contracts.
Useful as such devices are for getting children to take their turns unload-
ing the dishwasher, they seem unwieldy if not downright ludicrous in a
relationship which, if good, has always been far closer to O. Henry than it
has been to Clarence Darrow.

Now in the 1980s, the belief that marriage is the answer is very
much with us. Done now with the belief that it can save women from a
life of spinsterhood or work in the hat factory, done now with the belief
that a husband will, can, or should be expected to "save" his wife from

anything, we are nonetheless confronted by a new scenario in which marriage is pictured as the answer to "saving" a woman from life on the fast track by once again returning her to the comforting warmth of the hearth.

The hard reality is that there are no free lunches either on the job or in the home. There are, in each, times of lovely breakfasts and great joyous banquets. But day in, day out? No free lunches.

Getting married, having babies, taking care of a home can be an answer. It can be tremendously fulfilling. But like the job outside the home, it can never be *the* answer. In spite of decades of technical triumphs, your daughter's swim lessons and your son's band concert will continue to come on the nights your husband is out of town. Babies create dirty diapers as well as magic, and princes can turn into frogs. The utter loneliness of a week spent in the house with three preschoolers in late February is no worse but certainly no better than the loneliness of sitting alone at a typewriter trying to meet a deadline. Changing one's title from "housewife" to "working mother" will not change what it is you are going to have to do when the chips are down.

But changing how you do it and how you think and feel about yourself while you are doing it, and being sure that you are doing what you are doing because you want to and not because it is the decade's current "answer," *will* make a difference.

Instead of pretending that housewives didn't—and don't—exist, it might be more important to review what that job entails and choose from among its components which to keep, which to forget—or whether you want the job at all.

In the process it is important to remember that going from a life of independence to one where interdependence is a given requires certain adjustments whether you are a teenager having your first child at 18 or a businesswoman giving birth for the first time at 40. It's important to hang on to the fact that even the best-intentioned lists of duties and obligations will not work in a household unless all parties to the contract have some sense of ownership in it or caring about it. It is important to know that, despite scientific evidence on both sides of the question, most women do find that a baby has a way of "catching" them that makes it hard ever again to put the child second behind a career.

It is important to know that as a woman you will beyond doubt have to work for money to support yourself a large part of your life and to do that you will need skills, and that if you stay home for much more than a year your skills will need retooling. It's important to understand the need for adult contact and to know how the lack of it can make even the most enlightened woman overdependent upon her husband and children for support, comfort, and reflected glory. It is vital to remember that the need for fun never stops, nor does the need for time alone, and that both are vital for the maintenance of health.

I argued once, long and hard, with a professor of mine in graduate school about whether history was the spiral he said it was or the pendulum I believe it to be. As I see marriage, home, and family reemerge as a strong life choice for women, everything in me hopes that he, with his belief that we circle back and forth but rise always closer to perfection, was right.

4

The New Depression

"With So Many Options, I Won't Get Depressed"

On a long-ago Mother's Day my husband drove me to the hospital and my doctor checked me in because he didn't know what else to do with me.

What else could he do with a young woman who was married to a respected college professor, had three healthy, beautiful children, and was tired all the time? After all the tests had proved negative, what else was there to do but ship her off for a week's rest? No matter that she couldn't remember the last time she'd had any fun, that her few nights out each year were spent on the obligatory faculty bridge, which she loathed, instead of on the dancing and parties she'd given up when her first child was born. No matter that she rarely exercised and ate too many desserts. No matter that she'd lived all her life in cities and was now two hours from the nearest one. Never mind that she, a writer, had all but quit reading. Time for this lady to shape up and get back where she belonged.

Many years later, long after I had understood the reasons for my depression as a young wife and years after I had begun in my own counseling practice to help other women come to this same realization, I was dismayed to find myself feeling the unforgettable first signs of depression. I quickly reviewed my life: marriage, fine; children, two in high school and one beginning college and doing well; job, excellent, with the program I'd developed taking me all over the country, lots of speaking engagements, lots of interesting people, lots of chances to teach, write, counsel, and act out what I felt called to do. I was doing everything I'd always wanted to do and it was all so worthwhile. The words echoed inside my head. Wasn't this exactly what I had told myself fifteen years before when I had been at home with my three children?

Depression was the last thing I had expected to meet on the road to the top. But here it was again, filling my already full schedule with its emptiness.

I had, like many women in the 1970s, moved ahead rapidly in my career to "make up for lost time." I had, as Meg had said, chopped wood and toted many, many buckets of water. Yet here I was with those bad old feelings again. About this time two of my colleagues were experiencing the same feelings. We compared notes. Our lives, we decided, were almost the exact opposite of what they had been as full-time housewives. And yet, in their imbalance, they were identical.

Human beings need equilibrium, that balance between love and work, rest and activity, nurturing and being nurtured, male and female, dependence and independence, learning and teaching. But the things with which we fill our lives do not automatically provide this balance for us. Marriage alone does not provide it. A job alone does not provide it. Children most assuredly do not provide it. When we count on any of these things by themselves to provide the stasis we need, we are asking not only for disappointment but for the depression that almost inevitably will follow.

Our journeys to depression often begin in such benign ways: What could be more fulfilling than the nurture of children? What could be more rewarding than a meaningful career? What could be better than having both, or having it all?

Yet all of these activities carry in them the seeds of destruction if they become so all-encompassing that they are allowed to obliterate us in the process. As we have seen, self-sacrifice is a noble but tricky posture. It is one in which the slightest imbalance can push you over the edge into that place where you have so lost your self in the doing of your thing that you are unable to function effectively on behalf of that self or of anyone else—or, ultimately, the thing itself. (This is why "doing your own thing" in the seventies proved to be so unfulfilling. It never said anything about that necessary first step: Be who you are.)

Almost without realizing it, the loving, caring mother can find all of her days beginning to be a thousand hours long until on one of them she is finally too tired to thaw the hamburger. Caught in the demands of her job, the working mother can find almost overnight that it has turned from something she enjoyed to a nightmare from which she cannot awaken.

A woman on Long Island writes me this piece of wisdom in a letter which says it all: "When you focus on one part of your life to the exclusion of all others, you tend to forget the different facets of your personality and you lose your identity." You become so busy *doing* that you lose your *being*.

Thistles in Paradise

The young reporter from the *Boston Globe* kept interrupting me, saying she couldn't believe it. We were sitting over coffee as I told her about my work with women in the Midwest. I mentioned the loneliness and alienation felt by the housewives, the fact that the highest incidence of depression occurs among women in rural America, and that mid-American housewives have been for decades the largest subgroup of drug users.

"But what does anyone have to be depressed about out there?" she said with that sweep of the hand that easterners often use to indicate the "wasteland" between New York and Los Angeles. "It's all so peaceful."

The twin myths that (1) rural peace guarantees freedom from depression and (2) all women in mid-America are Norman Rockwell–

type moms who bake sugar cookies all day without a concern in their heads contrast sharply with reality. In truth, small-town America is a fascinating and frustrating juxtaposition of pioneering *chutzpah* and Calvinistic no-no. On one hand the very nature of the place demands and produces women with an inborn strength rarely seen elsewhere. On the other, the small-town ethos of conservatism and the belief that change must come slowly, if at all, makes new ventures not only suspect but highly vulnerable. (In my own work with women in the early 1970s, it was only after I had shown my personal commitment to the concept of family as well as to that of personal growth for women that the angry phone calls stopped coming and the tired jokes stopped being made to my husband about me.)

The sheer geographic isolation of much of small-town America makes it a fertile breeding ground for depression. Separated physically as well as emotionally from others with similar interests, women can often feel the way one Wisconsin woman described: "When the first snow falls each winter, I feel as if I've died and they've just put the sheet over my face." As she spoke, I felt a momentary pang as I remembered how, as a young mother, I had dreaded that moment each autumn when my husband removed the screens from our doors and began pounding in the storm windows. It had always reminded me of coffin nails.

For the woman who has grown up in rural America, the temptation to "make a break" for the city usually peaks at about age 18 and again in her mid-thirties. The comfort of living where everyone knows and presumably cares about her is weighed against the scary feeling that she may, as many women put it, "die before I have lived." The potential for feeling empty if she stays and lonely if she goes creates an ambivalence that can in itself produce depression.

Others of us are urbanites who have found ourselves living in small towns because that's where our husbands grew up, work, or retire. For us, the move from a place where such basic amenities as good libraries, dance studios, art museums, and delis are a given reinforces our sense of psychic isolation and the depression that comes from feeling not only out of step with others but somehow ungrateful for what one does have. Even though a small town does provide a slower pace of living and a greater sense of safety, these are counterbalanced for some women by the lack of opportunity for them to work at anything meaningful outside their homes or for enrichment activities for their children. (One of my students, a bright, articulate woman from Kansas, once likened her local library to a thrift sale after everyone has cleaned out Grandma's attic! After taking my class, she and two friends began assembling a collection of paperback books of interest to women, and she now provides other women in her community a sort of lending library and mental health resource center.)

As more and more families choose to leave the urban "jungle," some discover that there are also thistles in paradise. Some are shocked to find that many of the issues they had thought long laid to rest are still alive and unwell in mid-America.

A 47-year old woman wrote that she had just moved from Michigan to central Missouri thinking the last word had been said on a woman's right to make life choices for herself. She was horrified when she went to the first meeting of a local women's club to find herself sitting on what she termed "a powder keg of isolation and anger. I felt plunged," she said, "back into the pain I thought was over forever."

Where Men Are Men and Women Are Wives

If there is any place in America where women "have it all," it is in the millions of homes that make up the sprawl called suburbia, those places called St. Clair Shores and Edina and Lake Forest and Bellevue which line the lakefronts, encircle the major airports, and roar up one coast and down the other before sweeping across mid-America in a tumble of malls and condos and industrial parks.

Here live the women who have been on the forefront of the changes in family life. From this group traditionally have come the volunteers on behalf of the disadvantaged, the chairwomen of the charity balls, the docents of the museums, the scout leaders, the band parents. Here are the women who first read Dr. Spock (both times around) and *Passages*, who first discovered Similac and Donahue, book clubs and interior designers and spare time. These are the ones who first understood that to give your child the good life you must put that child where the good things are. And yet, the suburban woman is often a prime candidate for depression.

A lot of this has to do with the unreality of the suburban existence. It is the place in which you have received all that you were told you ever wanted. Whether that was the home—husband—four children of the 1950s and '60s or the home—husband—1.5 children—job—aerobics class—color consultation of the 1980s, and no matter how "good" each of these ingredients, it will not sustain you if (1) it is not what you want and (2) you do not feel a participant in it.

To maintain its veneer of perfection suburbia has been asked to sacrifice reality, and to present to the chaotic world a vision of perfection it has often extracted a hideous price from its occupants, particularly its women.

My own two years in the suburbs were some of the most painful of my life because of that unreality. I remember that the sun shone much of the time but it never seemed to warm anything. Instead, it seemed to provide only a cruel counterpoint to the joylessness of our existence. Conversations seemed to center, as I recall, on carpeting, crabgrass, and the chain link fences we were all in the process of buying to protect our emptiness. We walked our babies, we took our gourmet cooking classes, we went to parties on Saturday nights with our husbands, yet it seemed we came home as empty as we had left, needing always to buy more things to "fill" our lives. It was in my three-bedroom brick house in the suburbs of Detroit, surrounded by my loving husband, my marvelous baby daughter, my brand-new kitchen appliances, and all the spare time in the world in which to write that I stopped writing completely because I felt I no longer had anything to say.

A woman of 55 wrote to me last year about life in the suburbs: "Nothing's changed here. We still go through life like well-groomed puppets, able to cope with everyone's problems but our own."

On the Fast Track to Depression

I was a member of a panel recently in which one of the other speakers, a psychologist, said that wives and mothers who work outside the home experience depression less frequently than full-time housewives. Not long ago I would have agreed with him and with the well-established research upon which he based his remarks.

But what I've seen happening within the past few years convinces me that the differential between the two groups is not as great as we might once have believed. It is not that the full-time homemakers are experiencing less depression. It is that the working wives are experiencing it also. For some it happens because the job only reinforces an existing sense of displeasure with self. For others the startling realization that having a job does not provide immunity from depression can give them a feeling of being trapped in a life from which there is no escape.

Nancy, who went back to work after her children were all in school, wrote to me about her job as an administrative assistant in a city planning office:

> It is, I suppose, a dream job. My bosses are relaxed and casual and pretty much leave me on my own. Why, then, do I feel ill at ease, tensed up, on edge most of the time? Why do I often feel like crying when I get home? I don't seem to remember details *as well as I should.* Looking back on my interview and the things that people wrote about me in my references, I'm sure my bosses expected more from me than I have been able to produce. *I feel really disappointed in my performance due to my own high expectations.*
>
> It's disappointing to me to notice what tiny details have come to loom large to me when *I once imagined I was capable of doing well on most anything I set out to do.* I find that this job tires me out of proportion to the time I spend on it. When I get home some nights I just want to go to my room, shut the door, and cut out the world. [Italics added.]

Nancy's story is typical of hundreds I've heard within the past couple of years. Like the other women, Nancy is driven by the same internal admonitions that nipped at her heels when she was home all day: Be perfect. Please everyone all the time. Try harder and, while you're at it, hurry up. Since no one can ever reach the goals of perfection and pleasing everyone all the time, the woman who holds them will feel a deep sense of loss, a sadness that she had "failed." This is another loss that can trigger depression.

The woman who returns to work after several years at home often experiences an initial "high" that comes from feeling wanted and needed by Important Others. There is often the feeling that, great as it is to be back on the job, you will stand—or sit—willing, ready, and able to do whatever is asked of you.

It is not long, however, before the rift between what you are doing and what you believe you are capable of doing becomes painfully clear. When someone comes into the office during a time when most of the staff is gone, looks right at you, and asks, "Isn't anyone here?" you are hit with mixed feelings. Initially there is the hurt in realizing that, in your position, you aren't "anyone" to lots of people. That is followed by the even more frightening realization that since you can't get the travel budgets to balance or have not yet put this branch office on the map, perhaps you really aren't anyone.

"It Hurts Too Much to Cry"

Depression can strike with the sharp pain of a 1:00 A.M. awakening, or it can wash over you on a day when you take a hard look at your life and are overwhelmed by the emptiness of it. It can come on slowly, without your even noticing that it's been forever since you've really felt good or since you've been excited about anything. It can take the form of a terrible tiredness or chest pains or heart palpitations or anxiety attacks or headaches. It can make you want to pull up the blanket and sleep forever, or it can awaken you at four o'clock every morning with a fear that is nameless yet so real that your body aches.

Sometimes it makes you want to cry, but other times you hold in the tears because you know that if you ever started crying you would never stop. Sometimes you don't feel like crying. You are just hungry, and you eat and eat until you realize that all the fudge brownies in the world—or all the merit raises—will never really fill you up.

Depression moves along a continuum from severe, where nothing has meaning anymore, to the so-called mild form. In the past, mild depression has been called "housewife blues," as if to dismiss its power. But there is nothing mild nor powerless about it. It is a tough adversary, and it can affect you whether you are a housewife or out on the job.

The pain of depression is deepened by the fact that, unlike grief, it does not appear at first to have a cause. The grief that follows the loss of a husband, a child, or one's health is no less painful but somehow more permissible to oneself and to others than a depression that appears "for no reason." Depression brings double pain because, in addition to its intrinsic feelings of loss, guilt, and worthlessness it also produces an overlay of guilt about feeling so bad when you "have it so good." Whether this "good" is a home, husband, healthy children, a challenging job, or a string of degrees, the fact remains that you must somehow bear the shame not only of being depressed "without cause" but also of being "unappreciative" of the benefits life has bestowed upon you.

For many women, low-grade chronic depression becomes a way of life. Walking, talking, on the job, raising children at home, these women go through the motions of life in a sort of perpetual gray fog. This depression was best described by one of my first clients: "It feels like nothing is really wrong, but nothing is really right either."

The Enigma of Depression

Although depression has been around since the beginning of recorded history, there is still no consensus among mental health professionals as to its cause or cure. Once thought to be purely an "emotional" disorder, it has since shown itself to have physiological roots and causes. A vast body of evidence now suggests that many depressions have biochemical linkages.

Painful as depression is, it is often made worse by the agonizing search to find someone who will work with you on finding your way out of it. At a time when you feel least like leaving your house, let alone conducting a major search for help, that is exactly what is required of you. At a time when the very last things you want to do are move and think, those are the first two things that you must do.

First, you must move off dead center. Depression feeds on itself and deepens rapidly. If you break your leg, you do not sit around questioning whether or not you have a "right" to hurt. You know that you do and you get busy trying to get better. Do the same with depression; limping along in a gray fog, hoping it will be gone when you wake up tomorrow, is as foolish as limping along on an unset leg. Depression never comes without reason, and the reasons can range from a chemical imbalance to the loss of a parent in childhood, an idealized self-image that you can never live up to, or an idealized vision of a husband that he can never live up to. They can range from the feeling of having no control over your life to boredom, loneliness, and isolation. Depression can be triggered by surgery, no matter how successful it is, as a result of feeling helpless or in pain or, very simply, from some of the ingredients in your pre- and post-operative medications. Depression can still, after all these years and all these improvements, be triggered by the events surrounding childbirth. Depression does not follow loss in neat succession. It can erupt months or years later, and it can follow the end of a joyful event—such as your daughter's wedding or a promotion or a successful performance or the earning of a degree—just as surely as it can follow sadness. Loss is one of depression's prime triggers, whether it is loss of a person, a dream, or a goal for which you have worked.

Since depression is made up of things such as guilt, fear, anger, and loss, it is natural to feel those things when you are depressed; do not beat yourself over your head with your own symptoms by labeling yourself "bad," "ungrateful," or "weak."

The important first step in depression is to make an appointment for a thorough physical examination with a doctor you like and trust. If there are organic causes for your feelings, attend to them. If there are not, do not leave without discussing your feelings honestly and frankly with your physician. Under no circumstances settle for a physician who does not seem to understand that depression is a wily adversary seldom given to control by a single drug prescription or a single lecture about keeping one's chin up and thinking of all the others worse off than you. Seek a second opinion immediately if these are the only palliatives offered you.

Never simply tell your doctor you can't sleep and then accept a prescription for sleeping pills; as depressants, sleeping pills will only drive you further into depression. Antidepressants and other medication should only be accepted if you feel sure your doctor understands the complexities of depression or is willing to work in concert with someone who does. Never let anyone tell you that depression is "part of menopause" or that "it's natural for mothers of young kids to feel depressed" or that a fast-track job will lead you to depression.

Although "talking cures" for depression have come into disfavor in the past few years, to omit talking about your feelings during depression can be as counterproductive as doing nothing but talking. As you search for a person to talk with, remember that it must be someone outside of your immediate family. Your family is already too confused about/concerned with/angered at/uninterested in your depressed state to be of real help. Seek out a mental health specialist. If you don't know where to find one, ask a professional you trust. If you don't know anyone to ask, look in the Yellow Pages of your phone book under Mental Health Counseling or Services. Try to find someone who is trained to help you think through your life situation to the point where it begins to make sense to you again and you can begin to make some decisions about it. This person should also be able and willing to refer you to other professionals as the need arises and should be aware of the many facets of depression. If at the end of your first session with your counselor you feel any doubt about him or her, look elsewhere for help. Although you should not necessarily expect to feel better after the first session, you should have a sense that you can work with this person and that she or he is not only fully qualified but also recognizes that human beings do not fit neatly into little boxes marked "middle-aged," "career woman," or "young mother."

Any discussion or treatment of depression is not complete without an awareness of the powerful impact that exercise of any sort has upon mood. Excellent studies now show that daily exercise of any sort—even walking—releases some of the brain's natural tranquilizers (endorphins) and helps to restore a sense of well-being. Dramatic improvement has been reported among women who have done nothing more than add exercise to their daily routine; many of us can note a measurable change in our level of functioning after no more than three days without exercise. An adjustment in eating habits may also provide improvement or actual release from your depression. Many of us, by trial and error, discovered that the elimination of sugar from our diets has had profoundly positive results. You may also find, with the help of a nutrition counselor or a specialist in behavioral medicine, that other life changes are helpful to you. Many women have found, for example, that the addition to their lives of regularly scheduled relaxation breaks such as that described in *The Relaxation Response* by Herbert Benson has been of significant help.

Depression, by its very nature, pulls you into lethargy until you are tempted to sit and do nothing. At this time as no other in your life it is important, therefore, to keep to a routine simply to keep moving. Make yourself eat three meals a day even if you are not hungry. Choose something light and nourishing like a piece of fruit. Don't expect it to taste good; just eat it. On the other hand, if you have been overeating, make yourself go back onto three meals a day. Allow yourself one treat at each of two meals but after that, each time you want another treat, drink a glass of water. These are temporary measures and may be modified as you recover from the depression, but for the time being they provide a sense of stability in your life and, by the very nature of the routine, assist in your recovery.

During depression it is vital that you nurture yourself and, as much as possible, allow yourself some treats. Ruthlessly cancel or cut out everything in your life that is not absolutely necessary. If you have a family, do what you feel you have to to care for them. If you work outside your home you will have to decide what your job provides for you economically and psychically and then weigh the results of your decision. Perhaps your job is the one thing to which you look forward. Perhaps it is an economic necessity. If so, then you will continue. But if getting out of bed in the morning to go to work is more than you can attempt right now, take a leave of absence, as you would for a broken leg. If a leave is not possible in your job, you may have to consider quitting until you are able to restore balance to your life.

If things you formerly enjoyed seem meaningless to you, know that it is because, for the time, they are! It is as simple as that. Do not worry that you will never again be interested in them. Maybe you will and maybe you won't, but hang on to the knowledge that, though it doesn't feel like it now, you will be interested in something again. Meantime, search out something you would enjoy doing. This may be the hardest thing of all for you to do because you may not be able to remember when anything was fun. If you can't think of anything you would enjoy doing now, think back to a time when you did enjoy something, and do that. If that seems too hard to manage right now, continue your exercise and try again in a week.

It hardly seems fair, given the pain of depression, that we should have to work so hard to overcome it, but it is often *this work itself that effects the cure*. Whether the work is that of finding a competent professional to help you, the realignment of your life balance, daily exercise, or the discipline of diet, it is work. But work done to move through and beyond depression offers big payoffs. If you are willing to do that work, you will understand, maybe for the first time, how precious life is, and you will never again be bogged down worrying about what "they" say or what "they" think. You will feel more loving toward yourself and, as a result, others. Your health and your appearance will improve because you will begin to take care of your whole self, and you will have more fun because you realize that fun is one of life's necessities as well as one of its greatest pleasures.

My own interest and training in behavioral medicine convinces me that depression cannot really be treated unless the totality of a person is addressed: mind, body, *and* spirit. In most of the women with whom I've worked over the years, depression has appeared to be a denial of spirit. It has seemed to be a turning away from who they were meant to be (or once were) into who they think they should be. It has seemed a very deliberate, although usually unplanned, destruction of the life that had been born inside of them.

Recovering Our Being

Nancy wrote to me again about her continuing struggle with her job: "I keep remembering your advice 'just be yourself,' but it doesn't seem to help much because my next thought usually is 'Who or what is that self?'"

Within the past decade the examination of the self has gone from being sinful to being sacred. In the wake of these changes many people have been left adrift. Women like Nancy, who were raised to believe that to think of oneself at all was to be selfish, were suddenly asked to "find themselves" and didn't know how. Others, unaware that they had been "lost," suddenly began to have the nagging suspicion that they might have missed a beat back there somewhere. (A student once asked me whether, now that she had turned 26, "something wasn't supposed to be happening.")

The search for self that began so hopefully has taken on an ominous life of its own. Because the process seems so complicated and mysterious, many women are tempted to give up before they begin: better just to ignore the whole thing, they reason, and live with the familiar pain. For others, the suggestion that not to poke around in one's life is not to have lived persuades them that perhaps they are not as happy as they thought they were.

The search for one's self is not so much a one-time event as it is a lifelong activity. It is not one giant swoop into the morass of your life but a daily sense of in-touchness with yourself and your environment. You do not have to become a junior Freud. Look to the reality of your life and you will probably find most of what you are seeking. What has worked for you before? What has bombed? How do you feel about——? If *that* worked for you then, how will *this* work for you now? If you feel happy, you probably are; there is no need to probe healthy tissue. But if you aren't, then it is time to find out what is going on.

The search for self must begin and end as it always has: within oneself. This can be scary! What if I look in there and there's no one there? Because you feel an emptiness in your life, you may think that it is *you* that is empty. But it is quite the opposite: it is precisely because you are "full" of something, something you are not allowing to express itself in your life, that your life feels empty. What is most often missing in your life is the person you were born to be who got lost inside the person you are trying to be.

The indescribable loss that we feel in our depressions is the loss of our selves from our own lives. We have lost our connectedness to the person we were created to be. Because it is you that is missing from your life, you will never be able to fill that life until you get your self back into it. You will not be able to fill it with a job, a marriage, an affair, a baby, a Mercedes, a cruise each spring or a hot fudge sundae with a double order of slivered almonds. These things are filling to you only when you are present enough in your life to be able to enjoy them for what they are and let them go for what they are not.

Balancing Our Doing

I grew up believing my mind was "me." Unless something could be de-cided upon by my mind, I believed, it could not be decided. My body, although it held "me" together, wasn't really "me" (except when I didn't like the looks of it). As for my spirit, that was something best left undis-cussed except in church.

When I experienced depression as a young mother, I thought it was something "out there" which I had somehow fallen into—a sort of carelessness of my mind that had allowed me to forget just how lucky I was supposed to be. I looked, of course, to my mind to cheer me up, and when it didn't—couldn't—I blamed myself.

Next my body tried to let me know that I was out of balance by making me tired (please stop and notice what you're doing) or giving me chest pains and headaches (please stop and look at your life), but again I assumed these were something apart from me that could be treated with a pill or a heating pad. Never once, in those years, did I real-ize that what was crying for help were the parts of me I was denying by the lopsided way I was living my life.

Years later when I felt again the beginnings of depression, I was a mental health professional myself. I'd come a long way, through train-ing and experience, to understand the intricate way in which our bodies, minds, and spirits are interwoven. It became for me, then, a matter of reevaluation: what parts of me had gotten lost again in my busyness?

To correct the imbalance I realigned my life to include time and space for all of me. I readjusted my diet to cut back on the sugar that had begun, again, to creep in. I started dancing again, looked up old friends I'd been "too busy" to see for years, started to play again, planted a garden, bought some goldfish, and called a halt to working seven days a week and instead began to allow Sundays to be the minisabbaticals they are. I began to feel enthusiasm return. Not surprisingly, as I bal-anced my life I felt more energetic and, even after cutting out some "im-portant" professional activities, I was able to accomplish more profes-sionally than I had before, when there was never a free spot on my calendar.

It is important to note that what I put into and took out of my life are not the point. The point is that each of these things had an interactive importance for that part of me which had been hungry for them because they had been missing. As a housewife, for example, the things I had needed to balance my life had been quite the opposite: *more* intellectual stimulation, for example, and *fewer* goldfish!

Play Is Not a Four-Letter Word

I was doing a workshop on time management for an office staff, and I had asked all the women to list what they do for fun. Later, as they read the lists aloud, I found myself feeling weighted down just listening: I became impatient for the workshop to end so that I could go out and play!

The lists were heavy with "worthwhile" things. There was lots of jogging and there were lots of exercise classes and bridge clubs and gourmet clubs and the attending of children's sporting events. Did this account, I wondered, for what I had seen in the group? All of the participants were well-dressed corporate women, yet there was something about them that had not seemed quite happy. There was about this group the same kind of generalized joylessness that I remembered from my years as working full time with housewives who were chronically depressed.

When I began my counseling practice I was amazed to find that most of my clients could scarcely remember the last time they had had any fun. To the question "What do you do for fun?" I would most often get a blank stare. Others would mumble something about having gone out to dinner a month or so before; still others would reel off a list of activities that was exhausting just to hear.

"But what," I would insist, "do you do when you want to play?"

"Recreation," despite its lovely meaning (re-creation), has come to mean things that are not always fun. Jogging is only fun if it *is* fun; if you do it for your health, fine, but then you will need to get your fun elsewhere. Playing bridge is fun for many, but if you don't look forward to it (or back on it) with any joy, why are you doing it every week of your life? Spending every holiday with family members you'd rather not be with, sitting for hours in front of a television set, going to the symphony with your friends each winter and out on the boat with your husband's friends each Fourth of July can be great fun, or they can be events that weave themselves into the fabric of an already empty existence.

At a time when an empty space on one's calendar smacks of laziness, many of us try to pack as much productivity into our fun as possible. If a contract can be negotiated on the racquetball court, so much the better. If time with a daughter can be spent while she's playing basketball, great, and if yet another Saturday out with the same crowd seems a bit boring, so be it. It is easier than thinking up something new to do.

But often, as you arrive home and think over the day or the evening, you wonder why you don't feel more excited about it. Remember the days—and nights—of your life when you have gotten home from something and have lived and relived the delicious moments of it? That is what play is: not obligation, not duty, not business, and not necessarily worthwhile. Not anything but sheer, pure fun.

Play is what happens when you laugh and cry and share and leap and dance and celebrate and feel light and happy. It can happen at any age.

It can happen when you are reading something you have come upon as you turn to leave the library stacks, or it can happen while you are reading the latest gothic that just came with the mail. It can happen when you stay up on your skis for the first time down the whole sparkling trail. It can happen while you are putting on white face for Halloween, eating by yourself on the top of a city's tallest building at dusk, finding just the right color yarn for your son's sweater, knowing you are going to pass your Spanish exam, making love a whole new way, canoeing on a September afternoon, drinking a *kir royale* at Monaco's Hôtel de Paris, or walking into your garden to find that the nasturtiums you've tried to grow for ten years because your grandma did have finally bloomed.

As girls grow up they want and need to be women, to take on the responsibilities and the prerogatives of women and to be full human beings. But the fully mature woman is the one who knows that within her is not only the adult she has grown to become but the little girl she once was who still likes to play and the teenager she once was who still likes to dance. Those parts of us do not disappear with age; they are with us to the day of our death.

When we ignore the little girl and the teenager within us, confining those parts of ourselves to a psychic prison, they will, in their desire to be free, force themselves out in distorted ways. If we allow them to emerge, they can provide for us the spontaneity, the laughter, the capacity for fun, and the pure joy that only a child can allow. These qualities can enrich our own lives and spill over with richness onto the lives of others. But when the little girl is not allowed to come out to play, she whines at the world through the voice of an adult woman. When we suppress that part of ourselves who wants to dance, we become the adult woman who can never get enough compliments and has to keep producing until she is exhausted.

We need always, then, to allow ourselves to dance! Whether the dancing is literal (with a partner, in a modern dance class, in an exercise class, alone in your own living room) or figurative (a joyous celebration of life's possibilities even as you sit in a wheelchair and marvel at the way the sun sparkles on the million dust particles, or as you lie on a gurney en route to the operating room and marvel at the good looks of the technician), and whatever the steps that you choose, it is vital that you let it happen.

I am grateful to my wise teacher and friend Joe Tobin, who helped me understand that the world is full of people and opportunities that will allow us to feel rotten *if we let them.* But, he said, the world is also full of other people who are waiting to hand us daisies if we let them.

As women we have to be willing to take the daisies that are offered us, without false humility. When they are not offered to us, we need to make the wholehearted effort to pick our own armfuls of them. And always, no matter what, we need to be free enough to run barefoot through them, stopping now and then to put one behind our ear.

5
The Beautiful Sound of Silence

"Talking It Out Will Improve Every Relationship"

Once upon a time in this country there were homes in which whole meals would be eaten in silence. There were mothers and daughters who never discussed intimate feelings with each other, couples who spent entire engagements just going out to dinner or the movies or playing tennis, and husbands and wives who would let whole days go by without meaningful conversation. And then, at the end of the 1960s, into this array of silences, there roared that decade's answer: honest, open communication—otherwise and previously known as "talking it over."

Rap groups began rapping. Members of encounter groups

began encountering one another in hot tubs and classrooms, and marriage-enrichment weekends became big business. Marriage and family counseling became a discrete profession, urging a life-style in which sharing would be integrally woven into the family system. Doctors and lawyers were encouraged to be knowledgeable about communication patterns, and clergy increasingly began to schedule and attend seminars to help them become leaders of support and growth groups within their churches. Consultants from the human services flocked to business and industry, helping workers learn how to let their feelings out so that they would not get in the way of a day of productive labor.

I was very much a part of this move to break some of the logjams of the previous decades in which bottled-up thoughts and feelings had served to trigger violent anger or debilitating depression. Much of my early work in counseling involved leading self-growth groups for women of all ages. I traveled back and forth across the Midwest helping people see that without good interpersonal communication, relationships, families, and whole enterprises can go sour. I talked with groups of Lutheran grandmothers in rural Wisconsin churches, with radical feminist groups on university campuses, with the boards of directors of corporations, and with social workers in training. I was pleased, mostly, with the things that happened as people began to get out of their roles and ruts and interact with one another as full human beings. Along with my contemporaries in the helping field, I saw real progress toward the American dream of loving family and harmonious workplace.

I don't know exactly when too much became too much, but somewhere just before or just after the decade turned again, it did.

It is not that there is too much communication going on: good communication is still in short supply. It is that communication has become too tightly defined, too narrowly circumscribed, and that, in this slim, watered-down version, it is said to be the savior of all of our relationships.

We have been taught to believe that, no matter what the problem, if we just sit down and talk it all out, using "I-messages" and all the honesty we can muster, we can make any relationship work. When it doesn't—and it often doesn't—we feel dissatisfied with ourselves, angry with our partner in the interaction, and disheartened that once again we have played the game by the rules and once again we have lost it.

"I'm Not in Love, I'm in Therapy"

On a Monday-morning flight to Baltimore, a man in his early thirties tells me about his weekend with his wife:

"We had a really terrific time together, just relaxing for a change. Then this morning she wakes me up about five and says she doesn't think we are communicating as well as we should be. After this fantastic weekend I'm supposed to get up and discuss something I'm not even aware of before I leave for work. The thing is she never just wants an answer. She wants this conversation, this discussion, this *process*. Hell, I'm not in love, I'm in therapy."

As I listened to his story, I felt sure that back in Pittsburgh there was a woman who was still feeling angry and unfinished about the morning with an anger not unlike that of all the women over the years who have wanted to share their deepest feelings with their men, only to have the men walk away. The 20-year-old suburban wife, the 30-year-old career woman, the 40-year-old farm wife, and the 60-year-old in the condo all share the desire to express excitement, fear, anger without being told to cheer up or shut up. Each has within her a store of more days than she cares to count when she has felt the terrible aloneness of unshared emotion.

"I used to hear my mom whine to my dad, and he'd never listen. I swore I'd never be like that," Ann said to me in class one day. "But when I try to communicate with my husband on a really adult basis, he tunes me out just like my dad with my mother. What is it with these jerks?"

Ann's mother had grown up believing that women should keep a low profile in their homes and not "make waves." She kept her feelings to herself. Because she was unable to convey them in an adult manner, they came out in inappropriate and ineffective pleading, which is decidedly unappealing in middle-aged women. Ann, on the other hand, had grown up in a time in which women had taken giant steps toward full personhood. She had been told, and she believed, that talking together was one of the major answers to having a happy marriage. The results, as each woman found, were equally ineffective. The old way of (non)communicating did not work, but the new can be equally disastrous if it is used in inappropriate times and situations. As women move toward the improvement of communication within their marriages, they must be aware that

1.   Communication involves more than talking.

2.   The expectations women and men have of communication within marriage usually differ markedly.

3.   The communication patterns of women and men often differ widely.

1.   Communication Involves More than Talking.

Interpersonal communication is a complex interchange in which words are only one part. It begins deep inside each of us with our own histories, experiences, prejudices, and pain. These provide the seedbed from which our thoughts give rise to the words we speak and on which another's words fall when they come to us. It is the vital "something" that connects us—or keeps us separated—on the deepest levels. If our life experiences differ markedly from those of the person with whom we are talking, the words can seem to be as foreign as if they were spoken in another language.

This is the reason many women have found the talk of other women "boring" and have turned to men to find the something "interesting" with which to interact. It is also the reason women in recent years have begun to find the talk of other women to be more satisfying than that of men as they have made an authentic merger of two sets of common experiences.

Sometimes just the sight or sound of the person with whom we are about to communicate triggers responses that shut down the exchange before it begins. Even before his wife begins to speak, a husband can close his ears if she reminds him of his own mother nagging him to clean up his room. Even the sound of another's voice can be a powerful determinant of whether or not a verbal exchange will ever get off the ground. One of the most effective peer counselors we ever trained almost didn't get into Women Helping Women because of the way her voice came across to the interview committee during her telephone interview. It projected such an image of insecurity that it was only the powerful persuasion of her references and her written application that convinced us that we should take a chance on her. A voice that suggests a dependent neediness can be a serious handicap if we want to be taken seriously or even be listened to at all.

A voice that suggests there is no one else in the world but its owner also can turn off further communication. As we adjust our voices to indicate a sense of self-assurance, we need to be careful not to be talked into overadjusting to the point of stridency. The choice of "new" words can also be a deterrent to communication if the words are not authentic representations of the person speaking them. If we feel strong in ourselves as women, we can use the vocabulary of choice, but if we adopt a quasi-macho vocabulary out of a sense of anger for past grievances or because it will show the world how "strong" we are, we run the risk of seeming as inauthentic as the woman who enters her seventies still using words like "hubby" or "little girls' room" to describe parts of life about which she feels less than comfortable.

Whether communication is effective and satisfying or ineffective and conflict-producing depends also upon considerations of time and place. It is highly unlikely that a person whose sleep is disturbed at 5:00 A.M. for some verbal communication will be as enthusiastic about the exchange as the instigator of it. It is improbable that a person who had made it home from work on the sheer hope of peace, quiet, and a hot bubble bath will at ride's end want to sit down to share on deep levels in a family conference. The stereotypical bedroom scene of the past, in which the couple's lovemaking is disturbed by the woman's need to discuss the children's report cards, has not improved measurably even if the scene now takes place on a waterbed and the discussion centers on whether each partner's "felt needs" have been met.

2.   The Expectations Women and Men Have of Communication within Marriage Usually Differ Markedly.

There is a deeply felt common denominator, of course: each wants his or her happy ending in which needs are met and love—however that is defined—is felt. But beyond that, the expectations veer sharply in various directions. They cannot be divided neatly into categories: they cannot be dichotomized by sex, sorted out by geography, or pigeonholed as to whether the persons involved are Depression-era, baby boomers, ex-flower children, preppies, yuppies, or none of the above.

The fact remains that within each marriage—because of the nature of marriage itself—there is one woman and one man each of whom has a set of expectations asking to be fulfilled. This need is so universal, so pervasive, that the temptation is to grab on to anything that promises to do the fulfilling. Most recently this promise has been made by communication, but, as we are finding out, the promise is not being kept.

- Betty, a full-time homemaker, says that when something has bothered her during the day she just wants to "go hide in her husband's arms" when he gets home. She wants nurturing, but when he walks in and she's in that mood, he puts on a false gaiety, tells her to "cheer up," and grabs himself a beer. She attempts, she says, to "hold off" her needs until "later." But when later comes, after dinner or as they are getting ready for bed, he continues to negate her need. She knows her feelings cannot be "fixed": she just wants someone to listen.

- Pauline and her husband both have demanding jobs outside of their home, and they like to share their day's activities when they get home. But, as she says, she has a way of "spilling out every detail, such as 'and then a new pimple came out on my face.'" He seems to be listening and she thinks things are going well. Then, at a later date, out of the blue he will tell her something very important about himself and she asks why he didn't tell her before. "Because you're always talking," he blurts.

Betty's husband expected marriage to be a safe haven from the "slings and arrows" of his job. He also had a vision of himself as the protector, the fixer. These two expectations come into impasse at the door when Betty (1) greets him with a problem (her sadness) when all he wants to do is rest and (2) brings him a problem that he cannot fix (when fixing is all he knows how to do with problems). Unable to talk about it or explain his own feelings, he does the only thing he knows how to do: he tells her to cheer up.

Pauline's husband is a sensitive, modern man who would defend to the death the notion of egalitarianism. In his work he has often spoken out on behalf of women and the need for equality of the sexes. He had expectations that his marriage would be a partnership of equals. But equality did not include for him all the pimples and nuances that Pauline provides, and, feeling insufficient to the task of being that equal, he retreats into the defense of silence and then later, in frustration, dumps his retaliation on Pauline.

Communication can mean as many things to couples as there are couples. For women the need to talk it all out can mean just that, or it can mean "Oh, God, how I want to get closer to you, and if this is the only way we can do it, let's give it a try." For men talking it all out may mean just that, or it can also mean "I'll talk and you listen" or "You talk and I won't listen, but I'll 'make it all well for you.'"

Verbal communication between men and women often gets tangled in the question of how-much-do-you-love-me? and it can break down under the weight of a misinterpreted answer. Candy very much wanted to take the Women Helping Women training course, but her husband had planned that she and their children would spend the month of July with him in Texas while he was there doing a consultation. When Candy refused to join him, he construed this to mean that she preferred the training to him. This confusion of individual events with entire relationships is at the root of the apples/oranges confrontation, which goes, "You love your work/child/friends more than you love me," and which, decade after decade, refuses to lie down and die.

3. The Communication Patterns of Women and Men Often Differ Widely.

The typologies of individuals are many. Psychologist J. L. Holland has shown that there are among us those who can be described as Conventional, Social, or Artistic as well as Enterprising, Investigative, and Realistic. As we have seen, marriages usually do not take place on the basis of personality profiles, and so it is not unusual for a person who is Conventional, Social, and Realistic to be married to one who is the Artistic, Enterprising, and Investigative type. When this happens, friction can and often does occur.

"Talk is cheap" is the motto of those for whom it is. They do not realize that for others talk is a form of lifeblood without which they grow irritable and lonely. For those who cherish words and what they signify, all the loving action in the world can become meaningless, and they are driven to seek elsewhere for the verbal assurance of being loved. Arguments about the relative merits of words and actions are futile since, as in so many other things, what is important to a person is what is important, and all the discussion in the world will not change that fact.

Some men don't communicate with words because they can't. The hidden ingredient in many a "communication breakdown" among couples is the fact that millions of men have learning disabilities. (Women have them, too, but they are more rare.) Many of these men, particularly those over thirty, have never had the condition diagnosed and may not even know of it themselves. Some know about it and do not accept it; others know and accept it but have never discussed it with anyone. Many of these men have a background—often secret—of classroom ridicule and failure as they grew up and struggled with reading, writing, and reciting out loud. Perhaps they were laughed at for mispronouncing words during a book report. Perhaps they stood to recite in sixth grade and found that everything had momentarily "disappeared" from their mind. Perhaps they knew all the material for a test but had difficulty expressing it in writing or in spelling the words in a way the teacher would accept when all the *d*'s turned into *b*'s and the *was*'s became *saw*'s. Now that these men are adults they protect themselves by being quiet, by having their secretaries check the spelling on their reports, and by staying out of discussions with their wives.

When communication breaks down in marriage, the first thing many of us want to do is to sit down and talk it over. If we can just sit together, we think, sharing our feelings, our poetry, and our pain, we will at last have broken through to the perfect relationship. Rarely, if ever, does it happen that way. Instead the morning comes and we are faced once again with the reality of our existence: one woman and one man with expectations and frustrations that do not blend as we had hoped they would.

Beyond Words to Reality

The first thing we need to do is rid ourselves of the belief that talking it over is the answer to every problem. Since words are often the problem in communication breakdown, it stands to reason that more words are not going to be the solution. If we want change to occur, we must take an approach that deals with the reality of the situation and not the fantasy.

First, stop and review the situation. Be sure you understand what is going on, where communication is breaking down, what the causes are. Make sure you know exactly what it is that you want to see happen. Sometimes "communication wants" get all mixed up with frustrations, angers, and sadnesses about other things. Sort these out and come up with some basic "I wants." (A time to talk before dinner, his input into party planning, a weekly family roundtable.) Then decide what you are ready to do about them. Remember again that no one else is going to instigate the change; if others had wanted to (or been able to), they would have done so already. Since you are the one who wants the change, it is up to you to make it. At this point, bring in the Wet-Towel Reality Probe.

1. Work with Your Husband to Cooperate in the Change You Want.

I have been continually amazed in talking with couples to find that many husbands honestly do not realize what their wives want. Because of differing communication patterns and experiences, men often misread their wives' signals. Because of vestigial feelings of not wanting to ask for what they want, some women send out weak signals. It is important to clarify the existing situation before going further. Without anger and at a time mutually agreed upon, talk with your husband about what you would like to change.

Pauline and her husband agreed to talk on a Saturday afternoon between four and six o'clock. Instead of cataloging her grievances, Pauline stated simply that she enjoyed the time they spent sharing their days' activities but that she didn't want to be hit over the head later with how much time she had taken if he didn't let her know he wanted to speak. He, in turn, stated that he was deeply interested in her job and wanted to hear about it but did not want to hear every detail after his own day at work. They were able to negotiate for an hour before dinner to share the day in which Pauline trimmed down some of the details and her husband fleshed out his stories without holding back anything to "whammy" Pauline with later. Later he said he felt he was able to be more "present" in the experiences of his daily life when he knew that he would be sharing them with Pauline. She felt that sharpening up her conversations also sharpened up her entire thinking process.

In thinking through proposed changes in communication within marriage, don't overlook the importance of alone time and together time for each of you. Think of his day and think of yours. Remember that balance is vital in everyone's life. Almost everyone needs alone time after first returning home from work. This first half hour should be empty time. If this is a time when both of you are getting home from work, picking up children, and getting dinner, a half hour of empty time can seem an impossibility. For the sake of your marriage, make it possible. Hire a helper for the couple of hours at the end of the day, change your mealtime, or ruthlessly cut out some of the activities scheduled for that time. Unless someone is critically ill and needs an immediate ride to the hospital, all conversations, problems, and concerns should be put on hold for a later time.

If you have been home all day alone or with children, it is tempting to greet your husband at the door to hear about his day and to tell him about yours. Don't. Observe the half hour of empty time, and you will find that the rest of the evening—and the relationship—works better than it ever has before. In thinking about time, negotiate with your husband: agree to trade alone time for him in exchange for times in which he will be fully there for you instead of half buried in the newspaper or an old movie. Exchange alone time for yourself for times in which you will be fully there for him instead of draped with kids. Pure half hours in which people can really rest or really talk are worth whole dayfuls of words tossed out and never caught.

2. Hire Someone to Help You Work on the Change You Want

Betty was tired of tossing out words that were never caught. "He keeps ducking behind a beer can and the paper," she said in describing her marriage. "He's a good guy and I don't want him to do anymore than he's doing, but when I'm down I'd give anything for him just to put his arms around me and let me talk it out."

Betty's story is one of the most common I hear. Another woman wrote about it this way: "So much rests on a man's seemingly total inability to say 'I love you.' His stubborn—almost so stubborn he would rather die, have you die, or have the marriage die—belief that to say 'I love you' would be to give away some of his manliness, his vital juices. My husband demonstrates his love—he supports me, buys things for me, does things with me—but he is simply incapable of doing what I most want right now. Simply sit down and hold my hand and say, 'Hey, babe, I love you.' No expectations, no power trips, no nothing. Just 'You mean a lot to me.'"

For many women, like Betty and the writer of the poignant paragraph above, the reality is that what they want will probably never happen within their marriage. Their husbands are basic noncommunicators. Attempts to change them are rarely successful, and pleas, threats, and more talk only make the situation worse.

In working with Betty and her husband I talked with each of them separately before working with them together. Betty's husband said that he loved her deeply but that on his way home from work each night he would feel his chest tighten as he would brace himself against what her "problem" would be when he got home. He said he realized that she had her hands full with the children and the house, but by the end of the day he felt so tired himself he could hardly move.

"I feel responsible for her unhappiness, and I don't know what to do about it," he said. What he does is to pull away: her desperation seems to drive him into manifesting his uneasiness in negative ways such as withdrawal, false cheer, or retreat behind the paper.

I helped him understand that Betty was not depending upon him for an answer but only to be with her when she felt as if she were "drowning" at the end of some of her long days. He began to see that by taking time for a hug (which, in fact, expressed his true feelings) and some quiet listening with no expectation of a solution, he could alleviate the long problem recitals that Betty had delivered, not because she wanted so much to talk but because that was the only way she knew to get his attention.

On Betty's part, she learned the need that her husband had for some quiet time when he first got home. She bristled when he suggested that her voice and the topics she chose were in themselves turn-offs, but she agreed to work on both. After listening to her voice on a tape recorder she realized that it had deteriorated into a chronic whine. At my suggestion she signed up for a speech course at the local community college. She next reviewed some of the subjects that usually caused her husband's eyes to glaze over. At first she resented working on this. ("Why," she asked, "should I become more interesting if he isn't?") I helped her see that becoming more interesting was important to her for her own sake. By selecting different messages and different ways of expressing them, women like Betty can not only improve communication within their marriage but also open up new life options for themselves. Our language often becomes a boundary that can circumscribe our lives. When we allow ourselves to get more creative about the way we use language, we find that we become more creative—and freer—in the way we live our lives. As Betty began to work on her voice and her choice of topics, she reported back to me that she felt more "alive."

"A funny thing has happened," she said. "Now that my husband is hugging me more, I find I enjoy it but don't need it so much." She reported that as a result of her speech class she'd been offered a part-time job as a receptionist in the college speech department, which she will take in the fall when her youngest child enters first grade.

3.   Handle the Situation Yourself.

When Carol heard me mention dyslexia in class, she stayed afterward. As we talked she seemed stunned.

"I feel as if you've just pulled a blanket off our marriage," is the way she expressed it. "It explains everything." She also said it explained some of the things that were happening to their seven-year-old son, who was beginning to have problems with reading even though he was a "bright little boy" who had done well in his first two years of school.

Carol's husband was an engineer. How, she asked, could he have a learning disability? I explained that learning disabilities are many and varied and are often present in males of high intelligence. To help Carol, I suggested she read Alan Ross's book *Learning Disability: The Unrealized Potential.*

When Carol came back to the university for an in-service, I asked her how things were going for her. She told a familiar story: "I was on the verge of divorce when I came to your class. About a month before we'd been to a marriage-encounter weekend, and by the time it was over we were having one of the worst fights of our lives."

Carol, a newspaper reporter, loved to talk. She loved to talk issues, philosophy, film critique, you name it. Confused and frustrated as to why her husband would not join in with her discussions, she mentioned it to a friend, who suggested a marriage-enrichment event. It proved to be a crisis point in their marriage.

Marriage-enrichment weekends or any other events based on talking can be excellent for partners who are communicators. They are disastrous to a couple in which one or both partners are noncommunicators. For Carol's husband, the expectation that he would "perform" by talking out his feelings was pure torture. Afraid that he would say something the wrong way, unable to articulate his feelings, he was terrified during the entire weekend. Unable to express this terror the way he wanted (he felt like crying), he did the only thing he knew how to do to protect himself. He walked out.

Carol loved her husband. Once she understood the situation, she evaluated it. Just as she could not expect a husband with a leg injury to jog with her each morning, so could she not expect a husband who had discomfort with words to join her in rigorous conversational duels. She began to see that her husband had plenty to say: he just said it—and showed it—in ways different from hers. She decided that she enjoyed her life with him enough to want to stay in it and to find conversational partners elsewhere.

If you are married to a man who won't or can't talk as much as you would like, it is important to go back to the reason you married the man in the first place. Are the reasons still valid? Are the qualities you loved him for qualities he still has and that you still value? What if you have grown and he hasn't? Do the good qualities still outweigh the bad? If the answer to these questions is no, then there are serious difficulties within your marriage that require you to seek marriage counseling. But if you still love your husband and cherish his good qualities even though you despair of his ever being a talker, enjoy his good qualities and find other people and places to fill your conversational needs.

Men, even the most sensitive, can seldom give women the exact measure of empathy that another woman can. It is important for women to have at least one and preferably three trusted women friends in whom to share and confide. From there it is important to go on to other friendships. It is trite but true that if you are interested in something, go where people with that same interest are. Just because your husband is not interested in Woody Allen films, fossil deposits in Idaho, or rosemaling doesn't mean that you cannot be. Be sure that your life consists of friendships with other women and men and children of varying ages. If you confine yourself to friendships with women your own age and interests, you will become "conversation needy." You will be so hungry for conversation that you'll put expectations on your husband, as did Carol, that no one human being can possibly fulfill.

4. *Leave Everything the Way It Is.*

5. *Continue to Complain about Your Marriage for the Next Twenty-five Years.*

If you choose to go on arguing with your husband about your conversation patterns without making any changes in them, or if you choose to let your anger at noncommunication simmer steadily throughout your marriage, it may comfort you to know that you are in a legitimate, albeit painful, type of marriage in which millions of other couples exist from day to day.

In the excellent classic *The Mirages of Marriage,* William Lederer and the late Dr. Don D. Jackson describe the participants in such marriages as the Weary Wranglers and the Psychosomatic Avoiders, but also acknowledge that these constitute "a considerable proportion of the American married population." The choice of what you want to do with your marriage—and your life—is, as always, yours and yours alone to make.

Daughters and Mothers and Others

In response to the call for "open, honest communication," many women have mistakenly assumed that they must move into a sort of buddy-

buddy relationship with their daughters to assure a strong relationship. Nothing could be further from the truth! Relating honestly to a daughter—or anyone else—does not require being someone you are not. If you are a "blurter" who wants to share with your daughter, do it. But if you are a private person, not given to sharing the intimate details of your life with others, don't be intimidated into thinking that the omission of these details will somehow leave your relationship empty. Relationships are based on the authentic expression of each of the participants in that relationship. Sometimes this means that one of the participants is a talker and one a listener. Sometimes it means that both talk with wildly waving arms and wildly swerving minds. Sometimes it means that both sit in silence enjoying each other's company and being in that moment together.

Sally, a mother of four, speaks to me about her married daughter: "Now that she's married, I don't know how to be her mother." In this one sentence Sally had encapsulated for me the story of her twenty-one-year-long relationship with her daughter. It had been one of role to role, mother to daughter.

When we relate to the others in our lives role to role, as Sally had, we feel confusion and loss when our role is challenged. When a third or fourth person enters the scene we are confused about what our own lines should be. For mothers and daughters, this scenario can be particularly painful.

Sally had always been Bridget's *mother.* Even after Bridget had gone beyond needing her mother's help in dressing, eating, bathing, and toileting, Sally had directed Bridget's clothing selection, eating habits, and dating patterns. She had viewed their relationship as one in which she, the older, was *de facto* wiser and therefore in position to tell Bridget what to do. Now that Bridget was married, Sally was confused. She was wise enough to know that what went on in the marriage was Bridget's and her husband's business, but now that she was unable to direct Bridget's life she did not know what else there was to say to her.

I helped Sally shed her mother role, one that should have been jettisoned many years before. I helped her see that she could, from this point on, relate to Bridget in the only way any person can relate to any other: as person to person and not as role to role.

The role of mother or father is useful when children are small, but it is one that needs to be shed gradually each year as the children grow. If it is not shed, the child's independence is blocked and the entire relationship is stunted. A mother who never allows her children to see her own pain and confusion, her own doubts and despair, as well as her own excitement, sexuality, and joy in living, is one who has deprived them of the most important thing she can ever give them: herself. A mother who denies who she is in the service of being "a good mother" harms not only herself but her children.

I was with a woman about my age as she met her son at the airport on his return from his spring break in Florida. She had previously told me that she was not able to "relate" to him anymore, that he didn't want to talk with her and replied to her questions only in "short" answers.

After the airport meeting I knew why. She greeted this 20-year-old man with a barrage of questions concerning his eating habits, spending habits, and dating habits before he had time to pick up his luggage. As his bags came around on the carousel, she picked them both up and carried them for him as if he were a three-year-old. She quizzed him about the condition of his homework and informed him that he would have to "get at it" that night before he unpacked. I was becoming increasingly uncomfortable being a part of this vignette, and I could only imagine what this homecoming was doing to this man who had so recently come from a time of fun and relaxation in the sun.

Going Around in Circles in Circles

Some of us who were housewives and mothers in the 1950s and '60s often ask each other, "Where were you when I needed you?"

There was very little sharing of feelings going on in those years. Women got together, yes, but the coffee parties were usually times of sharing who knew of a better diaper service, pediatrician, or chocolate frosting recipe. There was mild complaining but mostly the women smiled a lot; weeping was done alone. I remember coming home from such get-togethers thinking I must be the only woman on earth who felt tired and confused at times and desperately in need of a discussion about almost anything but babies.

Much later, of course, we found out that many of us had felt this way, and it was then that some of us decided to do something about it. It was too late for us—our children now almost grown and our lives going in new directions—but not too late to share what we had missed with the younger women who followed us. This decision to share was at the basis for my founding of Center for Women's Alternatives in 1971 as a place to announce, up front, that the "little" concerns of women were important and that if they were not dealt with they could turn, almost overnight, into bigger concerns that had the power to destroy families.

From 1971 through 1981, at the Center for Women's Alternatives, in groups called M.O.M.S. (More Of My Self), Beyond, Transition, Venture, and Golden Dialogues, my staff and I facilitated the self-growth of more than a thousand Wisconsin women. We saw housewives become free enough to blurt out their anger and frustration (even though they had "everything") and move from that frustration and anger to a strength that spilled over into their families. Often, during those days, husbands would come up to me and say, "I don't know exactly what you're doing in that group, but whatever it is, keep it up!"

We saw women in their forties and fifties become courageous enough to come out from behind their roles and share the hopes and dreams they thought they had lost forever, and then move out to make those dreams come true in their own lives. We saw women move from the raw wounds of divorce into the slow, solid healing that yielded new growth. We saw women 80 and 90 years old, who had not talked in years, begin to share memories and feelings in small groups in nursing homes as we affirmed them as people fully able to live until the day of their death.

Year after year our evaluations were excellent, and year after year we would hear or read of some new accomplishment that one of our "graduates" had achieved. Some, who had once been afraid to leave their houses, went on trips back to their ancestral homes in other countries or took jobs that required much travel. Some who had felt silly choosing to stay home with their children found that they were able to combine that choice with home study and come out on the other end with the best of both worlds. Some found that with increased understanding of what communication is—and is not—they could improve their marriage and avoid the divorce they didn't want but which they thought was their only choice. Some learned for the first time that life does not have to be either/or and that there are satisfying choices to be made within one's existing life that do not require tossing it out.

First with a trickle, then with a stream, and then with a wildly rushing river, the pent-up stories of millions of women demanded to be heard. Self-growth groups began to spring up and proliferate all over the country. Under the mistaken notion that where five or six are gathered together there is growth, women began gathering in one another's living rooms or in the lunchrooms at coffee break in an attempt to rap their way to happiness. When it didn't work—and often it didn't—I often heard about it. Hundreds of letters continue to come in each year from women who have heard about our work and want to know why our groups work and theirs don't. "We're doing the same thing," they write, "but ours turn into a gripe session and we end up back where we started." Other women say they feel worse after group than before. What, they ask, went wrong?

What went wrong is that what they are doing is not the same as what we have been doing in our groups. The difference between a group that facilitates the growth of its members and one in which people just recycle pain is subtle yet powerful. The mistaken belief that "if I just talk long enough I'll get well" is at the heart of the confusion. Unless talk is guided by someone who can skillfully reflect feelings and content, allow the healing of both anger and silence, and bring the group to a satisfactory closure at the end of each meeting, it becomes little more than putting on the tape recorder and listening to yourself whine. Unless talk is followed by some action on your part, it is just so many words.

The strength provided by sharing within a group is measurable. Women are well advised to take advantage of the opportunity for life change that a well-run support group can provide. But in looking for one it is important to be sure that it has the following components:

1. *A well-trained facilitator* with a degree in counseling, social work, or another branch of the human services with experience as a group facilitator.

2. *A theme or purpose.* Whether it is a membership theme (for newly widowed, for mothers of twins) or a content theme (help with life planning, how to overcome shyness), the group should have a reason for being. Groups which are so unstructured that anyone can talk about anything at any time are frustrating to their members.

3. *A nondirective approach.* Directive counseling has an important place in the repertoire of a counselor, but it is inappropriate for use with women who are moving into intentional self-growth. A group should meet you where you are and assist you in going where you want to go, not where the group or its facilitator wants you to go. If the facilitator suggests that you have been foolish in your prevous life choices and cannot grow without making major changes and then prescribes these changes, seek another group.

4. *A commitment to each person in the group.* This means that you, as a member of the group, can expect your concerns to be listened to and taken seriously by other group members and the facilitator. It does not mean that you will be told to shape up and quit complaining or that they will commiserate with you endlessly. You should have ample time within the group to talk out your feelings, but then you will be encouraged to respond to them in new ways that will enhance your growth.

Women who have moved from coffee party chitchat into a poorly run support group run the risk of finding the cure worse than the illness. Instead of feeling that something is wrong with them because the group has not worked, they need to look for another group.

Women can successfully meet together without a professional facilitator and share concerns in a way that can be mutually beneficial, if the following conditions are observed:

1. Each member of the group must have reached an understanding of what self-growth entails, preferably through her own attendance at a professionally facilitated group.

2. Each meeting of the group must have a theme.

3. Each meeting of the group must have a facilitator. This task can be rotated among members who have the interest or expertise to handle it or may remain in the hands of one person.

4. Meetings must not be allowed to revert to chitchat or hand-wringing. Empathy, reflection, and encouragement are the key words.

But finally there comes the time when all the talking, journal-writing and support in the world becomes just another crutch. It is a recognizable moment. When that moment comes, we must move beyond talking to action or it has all been lost and we can blame no one for our misery but ourselves.

Does It Really Need to Be Said?

Two of the most unforgettable times of my life were when I sat with a friend in silence listening to the magnificence of *Tristan and Isolde* and rode home from the concert in the same companionable silence, and the time when another friend and I walked through the beauty of an October afternoon for three hours with no sound but the crackling of leaves beneath our feet. I am not by nature a silent person. I am, in fact, a world-class talker. Neither of these friends are nontalkers: both are men who love words and use them easily and often in their life and work. Yet these two times of silence are among my strongest memories of total communication.

For so long women were told to keep silent. When the silence at last was broken, talking became one of life's most important tasks. It was important, first, to name and describe ourselves after being named and described by others for so long. It became important next to share experiences and validate them in the company of others who had had like experiences. Talking—and talking well—became the entrée to a delicious array of jobs and decision-making positions. It made the difference between a life in which all voices were baritone and one in which a mixed chorus could discuss everything from the news to neurosurgery.

But for many of us it has now become a time to rediscover silence—not the frightened silence of a woman who is afraid to speak lest she offend, but the mature silence of a woman who knows that there are many things that simply do not have to be said.

There is such strength in silence, and yet how afraid most of us are of it! One of the hardest things for my counseling students to learn is to let moments (which seem like hours!) go by in a counseling session in which not a single word is spoken. The counselor in training sweats profusely as she worries that the client might never again speak. What, she wonders, has she done to bring the session to this impasse? Silence is also scary to a congregation at worship (Has she lost her notes?) to a person on a first date (Let's go where there's some music) and to people in general (Let's be sure we have an agenda/card game/program scheduled so that we won't have to face one another across a table).

But silence is only frightening because it is empty. To get rid of the emptiness of silence all we have to do is to put ourselves into it. Putting ourselves into a silence means that we let our being stretch out toward the other person we are with. The reason we hesitate to do this is that we are afraid that if we venture out into the silence there may be no one there to meet us and we will be left hanging there all alone with not even a word to shield our vulnerability. That is a real risk. We face a risk each time we reach toward the full expression of our selves and our relationships. But often, if we truly put ourselves into a silence and stay there calmly, the other person will allow his or her being to move out in trust toward us, and together we can share a silence that is more full than we could have imagined.

My students have learned that if they can be strong in their silence they provide their clients with a precious time to think and to become in an atmosphere of acceptance. We who have stood in pulpits while the congregation shuffled their programs have learned to put aside our own discomfort and hang in there until the healing strength of silence becomes palpable throughout the whole room.

After years of silence women are now celebrating together their commonality through speech. But as we mature as women, we learn that less is more and that we do not have to list our accomplishments so much as we need to *be* them. Very few people that I know want to return to the bad old days in which women spent twenty years together in a club and never really knew one another, or when Father was the only one who spoke in the house or when mothers and daughters were alien to one another.

But in our maturity we need to let go of our fantasies about the power of the spoken word. We need to set aside once and for all the notion that we will find that one perfect other with whom we will be able to communicate on deep levels day after day after day to the end of our lives.

Just as sometimes we prefer watching television or knitting or doing library research to sharing deeply with someone else, so must we realize that our husbands or friends or mothers or daughters or sons might also at times prefer library research, fishing, or the chance to "alpha out" in front of the TV to meaningful discussions with us. We must learn to recognize communication for what it is in its totality: not endless talk, but a flowing interface of spoken words, silence, writing, physical contact, time alone, and time of being together. We must realize once and for all that we cannot ever have all of another person, for to have integrity each of us must keep a part of ourselves only to ourselves.

Only then can we realize, finally, that communication is not something we *do* in a relationship but that it *is* the relationship.

6

Finding Your Balance

"I Won't Be Taken Seriously If I Show I Care"

"Pardon me for sounding like a woman. . . ."

The woman next to me in the meeting room where we had just been negotiating a training contract wore a gray wool suit with matching opaque hose and shoes. Her leather attaché case was on the floor beside her chair, the papers pertinent to the meeting were on the table in front of her. It was midmorning break; the other members of the group had drifted off for coffee. This woman, who had met me today for the first time, wanted to ask me if I was the one she had seen on a television show earlier in the year talking about Women Helping Women, but she prefaced her question with a thorough and apologetic explanation of why she had been at home watching daytime TV.

There we were, two professional women facing each other over a meeting table while one apologized to the other for having watched her on a television show for women.

For so long women have apologized and explained!

- "I'm sorry the cake fell when I wasn't looking."

- "I'm sorry I'm late, but my little girl had a fever of a hundred and four."

- "I feel guilty for wanting something more in life when I have so much already."

- "I'm sorry you're [sic] not having a good time."

- "I feel funny earning more money than you."

I feel guilty that I want to be president of the company. I feel guilty that I don't want to be president of the company. I'm sorry it's raining. I'm sorry the road has potholes. I'm sorry. Pardon me.

Where does all this come from—this pervasive guilt, this feeling of being responsible for everyone and everything that happens, this need repeatedly to explain our behavior to others and to present to the world this neat package of perfection? And how can it still be with us in a time when we have so many choices about what we want to do with our lives?

It would be easy to say that it comes from a poorly developed sense of self or a fragile self-image or a lack of self-esteem or of having lost, somewhere along the way, that belief in the beautiful little child that we once were. The truth is that it is a wildly varied, and varying, mélange of all of these and more. Central to the mix, though, is the terrible—usually unarticulated—loss we feel for the lack of connection between who we think we are (or are trying to be) and who we really are. This sense of loss stimulates anger, but to protect ourselves from the pain of it we throw a blanket of guilt over the whole thing. Unable to understand and to separate out these feelings, we dispose of the whole mess by explaining and overexplaining ourselves. We do this ostensibly for the benefit of others, but the explanations are really to ourselves. Just as the teddy bear we hug symbolizes the self we need to comfort, so are the explanations and apologies we make to others for our actions really done to justify ourselves to ourselves.

The part of the woman in the meeting room that is concerned with "shoulds" says that since she is a professional trainer for an educational company, she "shouldn't be wasting her time" on a television show about the utilization of housewives' talents. She apologizes for doing it, thus weakening the very professionalism she is trying to maintain.

The part of my cousin Ozzie that is concerned with "shoulds" tells her that since she does not work outside of her home and most of her friends do, her meals should be more interesting and her house cleaner than theirs, even though she has never enjoyed cooking or cleaning. It also tells her that she should be thinking about going out to work even though she doesn't want to or need to do it. The hours she spends apologizing for what she isn't doing take away from the delightful, warm, and immensely interesting human being that Ozzie is.

Ozzie will be able to stop her apologies only when she realizes that who we are is more important than what we do, and it will only be when the woman at the meeting can come out from behind her briefcase and acknowledge to herself that nurturing is still very important to her that she will fully realize her true strength. Until we let the full expression of who we are out into the open, we will be compelled to apologize and explain just to keep ourselves going, no matter how "free," "strong," and "new" we think we are.

Just as women have found it hard to accept the fact that depression awaits outside the house as well as within, so is it hard to understand how this need to apologize and explain can still be with us when we have reached a time in which so many choices are available to us. Bruno Bettelheim, in a class on enhancing self-esteem in others at Brigham Young University a few years ago, explained the phenomenon this way: A time in which the relationships between persons and their environments, families, and other human beings change rapidly and in which there are few standard behavioral guidelines is also a time that can present serious difficulties for many people. The increased "freedom" that is abroad as a result of these changes carries with it the responsibility of making choices, a responsibility fraught with dangers of making wrong choices and thereby acting "foolishly." The result of such self-perceived "foolish behavior" ("I like being a housewife"; "I want to teach children"; "I don't care if I make a lot of money") can be a decrease in one's self-esteem and a need to grab on to, once again, what others say is the "right" thing to do. To feel self-esteem, Bettelheim said, we must know we are capable of making sound choices, have significant input into what affects our life, and feel responsible for our own self.

It is only when we finally make the decision to live out our essence—the person we were created to be—that the need for explanations and apologies will stop. But getting to that point can be a long, lonely road along which are lovely beckoning signposts that urge us to take shortcuts. Because we are human, and because we are tired, we look longingly at the shortcuts. How nice it would be if this were the decade where we would finally "fit." But the nature of creation is such that human beings never fit lockstep into the prescriptive advice of any of the decades in which they find themselves. For a few lucky people, a decade comes along now and then in which they find themselves so at home that all they have to do is settle in and enjoy. But for most of us the reality is that we must claim our own lives in every day of them or be destined never to live them. This does not mean that we are committed to eighty years of navel-gazing. It means that we must live with a dynamic in-touchness with ourselves and those with whom we interact. Only as we do this are we really free to listen to the decade messages and decide which of the "answers" we will take as our own and which we will leave to others.

"I've Found Myself, Now What?"

A letter from Cape Cod bears a familiar message: "Now that I've found myself, I can't find *me* out there anymore!"

The writer is a housewife and mother who spent several unhappy years believing that to help her family she had to deny all of her own interests. Then she took time to read, think, and get her life back in balance. Now, she says, it is very satisfying for herself and her family, she "loves" being a housewife and is happier than she has ever been.

"But now," she writes, "I look around and see that I don't exist! I've been replaced by one part Bo Derek, one part social worker, and one part president of IBM. Am I the last housewife in the world? Help!"

As this woman and many others have discovered, living out your life in a fulfilling way takes a lot more than just "finding" yourself. You can do a perfectly gangbusters job of "finding" yourself, only to look around and discover that you seem to be an anachronism! That can be scary. Why did I bother, you may ask yourself, when it's so lonely?

The housewife who wrote me from Cape Cod is "all dressed up" now but has "no place to go." She has found herself but she can't find herself "out there" anymore. Housewives are dead, she reads, but she feels more alive than ever before. What should she do now?

In Charleston, a woman working in a gift shop tells me that she is an education major, loves children, looks forward to teaching, and has, in fact, found what she wants to do for the rest of her life. "I honestly feel like a fool," she confessed. "My husband is in medical school, and I feel like we're acting out the great American stereotype: husband professional, wife teacher, dog and house in the suburbs. It's embarrassing."

A secretary at the Department of Education in Washington, D.C., heard me speak and realized I might understand what she called her "predicament." "I love being a secretary. I'm well trained. I'm well paid, and I'm good at what I do. But everything I read tells me I've got to 'advance' myself. I've looked at the materials, I've gone to a couple of seminars, but *this is what I want to do*. Why do people keep trying to tell me I'm not happy?"

In a class one day, a student told her story. "I was at a party with my husband and several other couples. A man asked me who I was and what I did. I said, 'I'm Loretta. I'm a wife and mother.' Then I started to cry. I want to be a wife and a mother, but I want other people to think it counts for something."

When you find that who you are is out of favor with the popular view of who you "should" be in the decade in which you are living, it can be very lonely. When I was in high school I was a tall, skinny brunette in a time when Frank Sinatra was singing about how pink and soft the girl *he* was going to marry would have to be. I hadn't even bothered to pick a silver pattern in the days when not to have a hope chest was suspect, and I had the audacity to like Shakespeare, write poems and essays, and get good grades at a time when any one of these three was the kiss of doom for a 16-year-old girl. The painful loneliness of those years is still a part of me—it was years before I could admit that I had not been asked to the prom—and a reminder to me not to be glib when I work with others on finding the courage to be who they really are. But as I have reviewed those years, I have learned many things. I have been able to see that, even though I was "doing who I was," I was still terribly out of tune with myself and my world. I used to think it was because I was "different" or "the only one," but I now realize that the missing ingredient was that I did not allow anyone else to know who I was. I had found what I wanted to do, but I was not strong enough to be who I was, up front, without apology, which in my case took the form of debilitating shyness. If I had done that, I realized later, there would have been many others who would have shared my life with me, to the benefit of all of us. (Years later a man who had graduated with me told me that many of his crowd had wanted to ask me out but thought I was too smart and too busy for them to risk my refusal!) We are all waiting, as Garrison Keillor has said, to be asked to the dance.

Defining, Deciding, and Doing

By my junior year in college I'd finally learned that if I wanted to go to the dance I had better be prepared to get there myself. But a funny thing happened on my way to being a solo act. Once I'd defined myself and decided how I was going to live my life and started living it and connecting it with others, I never again had any shortage of partners!

My own journey to self-esteem had bumped along in discouraging cadence for several years, and so on the eve of my departure for summer school at the University of Colorado, bold measures were called for. I remember that my roommate, Shirley, wrote the words "inferiority complex" on a piece of paper, sealed them in a little box, and hung it on the bulletin board. She announced to me that since it was in the box it could not be with me. Spurred on by her rudimentary (but highly effective) attempts at behavior modification, I decided on a "go for broke"approach to my summer in Boulder. As I packed, I whistled loudly in my personal graveyard. I came up with a *definition* of who I was (tall, yes, but fairly attractive with good legs; smart, yes, but with a great sense of humor and not a bad dancer), the *decision* to act out who I was (a person who liked to write, yes, but one who wanted to be in radio and TV, not an English teacher; a person who liked to work hard, yes, but also one who liked nothing better than to play), and a plan on how I was going to *do* it (change my major to journalism, start looking people in the eye, act as if I felt good about myself, and find some playmates).

The results were classic before-and-after. Without getting contacts, losing or gaining twenty pounds, buying a new wardrobe, or playing dumb (the standard prescriptions for women in those days), I went from a person who could hardly make eye contact with others and spent most weekends studying or wishing I were somewhere else, to one who finished school with the best grades I'd ever had and the most fun I'd ever known. The temptation is great to deride this simplistic formula. After all, it happened when I was in college. How could it be useful to an exhausted mother of four preschoolers or the woman readying her *vita* for the chance at an administrative position? My own subsequent life experiences and my work with hundreds of clients over the years has convinced me that the defining-deciding-doing paradigm is useful no matter what our age or life work.

This is not to suggest that self-discovery, self-esteem, and self-expression for myself or anyone else are one-shot events after which everything is "set" for life. On the contrary, they are lifelong adventures in which we need to be engaged each day of our lives if we want to live them. What I am saying is that unless and until we *define* who we are to ourselves and others, we run the risk of living our lives in painful ambivalence. Until we *decide* how we are going to take who we are and live it out in our life, it will all be just so much theory buzzing around in our head, and unless we actually *do* what we have decided, we may find ourselves lying down to die, wondering why it feels as if we have never lived.

Step 1: Defining

Women who try to live (do) their lives without having taken time to define themselves and decide what they want their life to be about often find themselves at high risk for depression.

The housewife in Cape Cod and all the other women who have chosen occupations that are momentarily "unpopular" must begin by taking themselves seriously. Until you do, no one else will. No matter how much others say they think keeping house or running an office are some of life's most important tasks, the reality is that they will not sit up and take notice until you start to believe it yourself. Women who wait for "society" to give the housewife or the secretary the respect she deserves are in for a long wait. Respect cannot be legislated. Women who have decided, once and for all, that a housewife or a secretary or a waitress or a teacher or whatever it is they choose to do is worth respect find that, almost overnight, they have it.

As I told Jerry and have told so many others, remove "justa" from your vocabulary and your mind forever. If there are any lingering doubts about this, they will show. Take time to examine the doubts carefully. Are you a full-time homemaker because that is where you want to be right now? Are *you* convinced that what you are doing at work is a worthwhile job? If not,why are you doing it? If you are convinced that it is, then state it loudly and clearly to yourself and to anyone else who asks. Self-definition is not a matter of putting labels on yourself. It is a naming of what already exists. My own definition of myself when I was in college was not a game of "let's pretend." It was an honest acceptance, for the first time in my life, of my strengths as well as my weaknesses.

Once you have successfully removed the concept and the "justa" from your mind, be sure you do not replace them with a laundry list of what it takes to do your job which you can nail people with who ask you what you do. A frustrated, angry person shouting out why she should be respected is pitiable, not admirable. No one is interested in your list! A job is a job is a job. If you know it, you will show it and you will *be* it. Women who are pediatricians and architects and agents do not spend conversational time toting up their job descriptions. Neither should you. If you are a full-time housewife, refuse to buy the myth that having a job outside the home automatically makes a person more interesting, or that certain jobs intrinsically produce more interesting people than do others. Interesting people find interesting things to do and make interesting things happen; work does not transform a dull person into an interesting one. A woman who knows who she is and acts it out is a gorgeous sight to behold, and she should let nothing deter her from her decision.

Next, define yourself. The world is full of people who stand ready to define you: "Nice lady of 60, obviously that 30-year-old man with you is your son." . . . "But we didn't think you'd want taps on your shoes because you aren't in a dance class." . . . "Well, what can you expect, look who she married." . . . Don't let them!

If you live in the suburbs, don't live up to the caricature of the woman who dabbles in this and that, talking constantly, saying nothing, buying everything in sight. Let the next bandwagon roll by without you; let go of a few of the programs and start looking to yourself for answers. If you live in rural America, remember that you live in the world as well as the small town you feel "stuck" in. Don't let others tell you what you like or don't like or what you are or aren't interested in. Don't waste your energy on anger; look around for others who want to share with you some of your life and enthusiasms. The pioneering spirit is alive and well in rural America, and you can be part of it by revealing yourself instead of hiding away because you feel "different."

If you are a housewife with children in school or a woman whose children are grown, or if you have no children, you are especially vulnerable to definition by others. What, people ask themselves, can be keeping her at home now? Implicit in the question is a second one: And why isn't she out doing something? If this is the position you are in, dig in your heels and do a strong self-definition. If you are home full time because you want to be, then that is your choice and you must not allow others to sway you from it. You are at particular risk of being viewed as a dilettante, a dabbler who moves from workshop to seminar without a thought ever taking root in your head. To counteract this, first be sure that is not what you *are* doing. If you feel some emptiness around the edges, it is important to take time to review your life and make some reconnection of yourself with your activities. But if you are among the millions of women who are happy to be taking care of a home and having some unstructured time, don't let yourself be swept up in the myth that to earn a place on this earth one must be incessantly busy with work defined by others as significant.

The number of women who have taken a job, gotten a divorce, or lined up to receive a degree in a major in which they had no interest because "everyone else was doing it" is frightening. If you feel good about what you are doing—or not doing!—do not allow anyone to tell you that it is not significant, worthwhile, or patriotic. The very fact that it is working for you is all the answer you need as to whether it is right for you.

A large part of defining who you are comes with looking people directly in the eye without apology or anger when they ask what you "do." I remember how ridiculous this advice sounded to me when a friend in her fifities gave it to me when I was 29. Not only did it seem to me to be proof that she was starting "over the hill" but also that she was hopelessly out of touch with my "hectic, modern life." But I also remember that I tried it out at a party—probably in desperation—on one of my few nights out that year. An attractive man asked me what I'd read recently. I looked him straight in the eyes, handed him my empty drink glass, and said, *"The Velveteen Rabbit.* When you get back with my drink, why don't we talk about it?" He not only returned with my drink but we also did talk about it, and my three kids and his four and his job as a musician and mine as a housewife. In the years since I began working with women, I've been privy to more tired jokes and comments than I would have believed possible. My most effective response has always been to turn the joke/comment/not-cute question back to the giver of it and ask him calmly but directly what he meant by it. Only at this point can real conversation begin. *How we define ourselves and act out this definition is the major determinant of how others perceive us.*

Step 2: Deciding

I still remember the warning I was given when I went back to work part-time after my third child entered school. I was the only woman on the block who worked outside of her home. I was warned that my children's grades would slip and that our family life would suffer. Years later, with mothers a given in the work force, echoes of the warnings given to me reverberate in the lives of women who attempt to move ahead in their careers a bit faster than others think they should or a bit further than where their husbands are in *their* careers.

Jane, a friend of mine, says that she has reluctantly come to the conclusion that her chronic low back pain is the result of the tension she feels each time she experiences a new success at work. She has scoffed off the warnings of both her mother and her mother-in-law that she must not get "too far ahead" of her husband, because she has always felt strong support from him for her work. But she now admits that she feels "sort of guilty" because she's had so much success.

"Sometimes now I won't tell my husband for a week after I get a raise or when I get a new account," she says. "I find myself keeping up a professional front at work and then backing down [sic] at home and pretending it's all just a one-time piece of luck." The correlation between Jane's psychic and physical pain is obvious to me. Until she can clearly decide how she is going to act out who she has defined herself to be, she will continue to suffer the pain. If she decides that her success really is getting in the way of her relationship with her husband, then she will have to make other decisions. Will she quit her job? Will she keep the job but let further opportunities for advancement slip by her? Is the job important enough to her that she is willing to risk the relationship to continue her success? If she decides that her husband does honestly affirm her success, then she will need to decide to get rid of her doubts or continue to suffer the results of her ambivalence.

The human organism cannot bear the pain of being told to win and lose at the same time. It cannot go forward and backward simultaneously; it cannot smile and frown at the same time. Choices and decisions must be made and action begun, or the ambivalence will manifest itself in illness of various sorts.

It takes strength to make decisions and it takes strength to live with the results of the decisions we make. That, too, is scary. But strength does not preclude gentleness, vulnerability, and the possibility of making mistakes. It does not ask that we go it alone. It only asks that we give up being weak. If we are to live out the lives we have been given, we must not reach for yet another script to follow. We must be strong enough to face up to who we are and what we are going to do about it.

The writing on the old poster is fading but the truth remains: "Not to decide is to decide."

Step 3: Doing

"And don't ever apologize for your decision!"

I don't think I will be able to forget the way my friend's voice punctuated the cold air as we walked along the lake in Madison that

March day I'd finally wrestled to the ground my decision to pursue a doctor of ministry degree instead of the Ph.D. that I and everyone else had expected me to choose. This colleague had helped me work through my decision-making process. It had been one that took me many months. (Along with others, I find it hard at times to practice what I preach!) Now that he could see that I had made the decision that I felt was right for me, he reinforced it with this command.

It was now time for the doing.

I have sat, over the years, with hundreds of women who have with great pains worked through their self-growth, have had their quota of "aha" experiences, have completed seminars on goal setting, and yet nothing ever happened. There comes a time, finally, when all the defining and decision making must be acted out or it is just so many pages sitting around in a notebook. It is not any harder to *do* than it is to define and decide, but it is also not any easier. Each step in this process requires risk, and the thing that we are risking is our self. If we lose that, we think, what else is left?

The reality is that we seldom, if ever, lose ourselves in the doing. It is in the nondoing that the peril lies. Doing can bring us into mistakes, into quandary, into sadness, into loneliness, but at least it will bring us into life. Not to do brings only stagnation.

Irene has been thinking about divorcing her husband for five years. She has defined who she is and what she wants in life. Her children are grown and she has honestly decided that, given the facts of the situation—a bitter, verbally abusive husband—the best thing for her to do is to leave the marriage. I agree with her. And yet, five years after the decision, she is still in the marriage, still unhappy, still seeing me from time to time to "talk it over." The prospects for her being in the same situation when she is 70 are very good indeed.

When I was a little girl I lived in Cleveland and my most favorite and unfavorite ride at Euclid Beach was called Over the Falls. After a leisurely ride through waterfalls and caves and gnomes and flowers, the machinery of this diabolical ride started your boat up an incline from which you knew there was no return. Up and up you went. You could look out over the park and see kids playing and eating saltwater taffy and riding safe things like the bumper cars, but you knew, down there in the pit of your stomach where all knowing takes place, that you were committed. You knew that soon it was Time. I don't know how they did it, but in looking back I've decided that the manufacturer of that ride must have known more about life than just how boats are designed. Because when your boat got to the very top of that steep incline it paused for just a split second—as if allowing you to think of what your decision to get on this ride was now going to do to you—before plunging you with heart-stopping suddenness down, down, down almost ninety degrees into a pool of icy-cold water that soaked your clothes, often scared you into wetting your pants, but always brought you back to the reality that you were alive and glad of it.

That is what doing is all about.

It's about "bewaring" answered prayers, and it is being sure of what you want because you just might get it. But it is also about the absolute, total joy of knowing that you have plunged ahead with this job/new house/love affair/baked Alaska/pregnancy/party for 500, and that, for better or worse, you are living out your life, never mind that others are content to sit by licking their snow cones and watching.

My friend's admonition not to apologize was some of the most valuable advice I've ever received. It was the impetus for my decision, within the past year, to stop apologizing and explaining myself and my life decisions to others. How easy it would have been for me to do otherwise! How many times since that day people have given me splendid opportunities to blubber on about why I did this or didn't do that. How many chances there have been for me to pick at the scabs of my old insecurities.

Life never fails to bring us the people and the situations that will permit us those doubts: I'll bet you're feeling exhausted getting ready for your daughter's wedding. I'll bet you'll regret trying out for that play when you see how much work it really is. I'll bet you're sorry you got your hair cut so short. I'll bet you're exhausted all the time now that you're head of the division. I'll bet you'll regret putting in that skylight when you see your heating bills. I'll bet you'll be sorry you paid seventy-five dollars for those tickets when you see the performance.

Sometimes, of course, they will be right. But when we allow others' doubts to bring us to our knees before or during the fact, we are giving the doubts and fears more power than they will have even if what they represent comes true in its worst form.

Self-Esteem: The Real Meaning of Power

Every few years words that have up to that point been good and useful lose their usefulness because they have become heavy with the weight of emotional or political overtones. "Power" is one such word. But because it is a word that signifies things which are so positive and life-enhancing, I refuse to quit using it. Power is the basis for the self-esteem each of us seeks.

I am sitting alone in the lobby of a hotel in Indianapolis near the registration desk, waiting for a friend. In front of me a tableau of power and powerlessness is being acted out. As the people come to the desk to sign in or check out, it soon becomes apparent to me that the costumes they wear, their age, and their sex have very little to do with the sense of power they project. I decide to focus on the women.

Here is a group of four well-dressed women in their forties, checking in for a convention. One argues with the clerk as she waves a sheaf of papers at her. A second calls shrilly to the bellhop to leave her bags alone until she's done, and the other two huddle near their luggage with an air of being lost. Judging by the appearance of their bags and their clothing, this group is made up of "power people," yet there is about them that air of out-of-touchness with themselves and their environment which spells powerless.

Nearby a woman who looks to be near 80 is checking out. Her clothes are not remarkable and her black purse hangs over her arm on a strap. Yet there is about her a sense of power. Here are others: two women with briefcases, felt fedoras, and good-looking wool suits. One looks centered and powerful; the other, in similar costume, powerless. What makes the difference? I am almost sorry when my friend arrives and I must leave.

The recent rash of books and seminars on power for women would be laughable if they weren't so dangerously off course. They have missed the point that was so clearly made in the hotel lobby and the one that we all know yet are afraid to say out loud. We can talk for days about situational power and positional power and hierarchical power, but when all is said and done we come to the realization once again that true power does not have any more to do with the size of your office, the color of your luggage, or the lettering on your business card than it does with the size of your breasts, the grades your children make in school, or the flavor of your potato salad. Each of these things *can* get you one or more of the things you may want in life—which may, indeed, feel good—but none of them separately nor all of them together can provide you with true power.

True power has everything to do with knowing who you are and being it, knowing that at any moment you could lose any or all of the things named above.

The word "power" comes from the root *poier,* which means "to be able," and it is only in the nurturing of our personal power—our to-be-ableness—that we can fully live. Each of us is born with our own personal store of power (to-be-ableness), but it can be buried under years of being put down, yelled at, or told we are worthless. It is only by defining, discovering, and doing that we can rediscover it and claim it as our own. Once claimed, personal power is self-generating; once released, it provides us with a lifelong store of the strength needed to continue our decision-making process and the freedom to do it in a way that is open, loving, and allowing of our self and of others. It is the quality that renews and refreshes us when we begin to question ourselves and our choices, and it is what enables us to say "I'm a housewife," "I'm fifty," "I'm going to go for it no matter what anyone says," or "I'm dying" without anger or apology.

How different this is from the pseudo-power strategies that demand of us that we dress, talk, and act in certain ways under some mistaken notion that this group of sound-alike look-alikes will rise to some other-defined "top." Things like offices, jobs, business cards, hot tubs, and Corvettes can be wonderful. But like husbands, lovers, youth, parts of one's body, and life itself, they are time-limited. This is not to suggest that we cannot enjoy them, but when we begin to equate any of these things with power and equate not having them with powerlessness, we miss what power is all about.

Women in the work force are beginning to share with me the irony of having finally shaken off their long-held "prisoner" stance only to be urged to take on a prescribed "warden" role. Claire, who works in packaging, tells her story:

"I was named manager of my division. I know this sounds crazy, but it has always bugged me that the secretaries had to take their breaks at prescribed times. How can everyone possibly have to go to the bathroom at the same time? Anyway, I decided that I would let the sixteen women in my division have discretionary power over their bladders and choose when they wanted to take their fifteen-minute breaks. I was just about laughed out of the division managers' meeting the week I announced it. They seemed to think I'd have mass anarchy, but I'd been under some naive belief that some of the others might want to try it. No one did, of course. That was eight months ago. Our production and morale are up and we get measurably more work done. We have a waiting list of women from some of the other divisions who want to transfer to mine if there's a vacancy."

As Claire and many of the rest of us have found out, when we use our power—and if we have it, our authority—to release the personal power of others, it enhances the total power of the entire enterprise.

It is very hard for some of my colleagues to believe that many women today do not buy into "power" games, not because of fear of success or fear of failure or because they don't know the rules, but for the very benign reason that they are simply not interested in either the game or the prize. They know that a woman can be just as miserable holding her Gucci bag and hailing a taxi to take her to a place she doesn't want to go as she can be in a kitchen packing lunches for a family she does not want to be with. They understand that getting on the fast track is important only if the goal at its end is worth the race.

I would be among the first to say that women must know the rules of the game, must understand that working for a living is now a fact of life not only for men but for women, and must realize that without salable job skills, consistently updated, we put ourselves in lifetime jeopardy.

But along with job skills, each of us must develop skill in decision making so that we can respond to the options open to us throughout our lives from a position of personal power rather than from the decade's lockstep.

From Wimp to Bitch and Beyond

For many women today, the skewed versions of power as articulated in "power books" have produced a skewed search. Every year in Women

Helping Women classes are several women who are filled with such anger that they can hardly handle the material we are dealing with because it triggers and retriggers in them their anger at the lives they have been leading.

Elsa, 37, is in her second marriage, has two sons, and is thinking of going on to be a social worker. She was an excellent student in my classes, but her anger kept getting in the way of her classroom performance. I suggested we talk.

"I was a doormat in my first marriage," she said. "This time I decided it was going to be different. I'm going to call the shots before he gets a chance to. I'm my own person. I'm in charge of my life, and everyone else can shove it if they don't like it."

Elsa exemplifies the women who have misread what power is about. As she talked, and as we had seen her in class, she looked anything but powerful. Often on the edge of her chair, always ready to correct us if we slipped into what she thought was a comment that "downplayed" women, quick to offer derision to the three women in the class who were full-time housewives, she did not have the strength and quality of centeredness that characterizes the person who is really in touch with her own power.

After we had talked, I agreed to work further with Elsa in finding the true power within her which she had not to this point been able to unlock. As we made plans for doing this, she acknowledged that she had been unable to make the switch from powerlessness to power. In a moment of charming vulnerability she admitted, "I guess I'm destined to be either wimp or bitch."

I worked with Elsa for five sessions on releasing the leftover anger from her first marriage, which she had never fully expressed and which was blocking her ability to deal with the here and now of her life. Although she had joined a support group after her divorce, the group was not designed to be therapeutic, so there had been no structured provision for the release of her anger and the grief she had felt at the dissolution of her marriage. As we worked together, we both realized that there was more work to do, so I referred Elsa to a therapist in her hometown, where she could continue to work when she left the university.

Next I used one class session to explain to Elsa and the other students how a skewed vision of what power is can actually take women from powerlessness back into powerlessness, leaving them with a chronic anger and frustration that spill out not only into their lives but into the lives of those with whom they interact. I explained that the mistaken interpretation of what power means can take women from not being in charge of their own lives (powerless wimp) into taking charge of others' lives (powerless bitch) without ever getting to where they really wanted to go: being able to take charge of their own lives (powerful woman).

On page 80 of Sheldon Kopps's marvelous book *If You Meet the Buddha on the Road, Kill Him!*, he speaks of power as the ability to articulate one's being but warns of its misuse when we attempt to have power over others. He writes: "If the realm in which power is to be realized is turned toward the creative possibilities of the self, then the excitement and the joy becomes possible. But, if this freedom is experienced as *power over others*, both parties will be trapped."

The woman who busily concerns herself with everyone else's life, who orders others around and decides for others what they should do, reflects the tragic emptiness and powerlessness of her own life. Because she cannot face, or handle, what is inside her, she turns to the infinitely easier task of handling others' lives, thereby effectively ensuring that she will never have time to live out her own.

Women who aren't able to release their own personal power find that their powerlessness provides a dangerous legacy to their children. In powerlessness is the message to daughters that women need either to find someone to care for them or someone to vent their anger on. To sons the legacy of powerless mothers is that men are in the world to be cared for and to dominate, thus perpetuating the pain of the past.

A mother who is able to provide for her daughters and sons the vision of what real power and strength are all about and allows them to choose how they will act it out in their lives is one who does not have to worry about how they will "do." Such women do not need to talk about whether their daughter should be a mother or an engineer but can affirm her decisions to be either, neither, or both. She does not need to talk about whether her son will be strong or gentle because she knows that one is intrinsic in the other.

A student of mine from Boston, a housewife, part-time paraprofessional counselor, and one of the strongest women I've ever met, wrote of her feelings about power and women and the way it is for her:

In the search for something called "power" women can lose sight of the fact that many of the so-called "feminine qualities" are the ones that would benefit humanity. Sensitivity, perception, nurturing, skill at interpersonal relationships are not the only things but they are also not "nothing." Why aren't they considered to be "power"? Perhaps it is time for us to show that they are. It is time to develop them and incorporate them into the life of the world as well as the life of the home. . . . We need to communicate to each other our abilities as women rather than apologize for them. . . . I am well aware of the struggle of most women just to learn that they can do something worthwhile . . . but I worry that women have somehow lost the importance of working together, each person in her own way, with her own abilities, for the benefit of all. I worry that in their anger . . . [women] have lost a sense of their uniqueness. . . . Until we can believe in ourselves and our value *as we are,* until we can equate power and success with the living out of our lives, instead of as extrinsically designed goals . . . we will not have the power to accomplish things we consider to be important. . . . It will not be an easy task. . . .

But who among us really wants to consider the alternative?

7

Flowing with Life

"From Now On I'll Only Do It My Way"

As I walk toward my classroom this morning I know beyond all knowing that in the course of this day someone in my class will say: "They're not going to tell me what to do!"

It is the day we are doing our mock job interviews, a time in which the women in my class practice what it will be like when they go out to apply for a job. They have been told to dress for interviews. Yet there will be at least one among my students who holds stubbornly to the vestigial hope, so dear to all our hearts, that the world will permit her to be totally and completely herself.

She will come to the interview in either bare feet (if it is summer) or a sweatshirt saying something bold and inappropriate (if it is winter).

She will not have her résumé with her and she will, with appealing bra-
vado, honestly believe that she will be able to get not only the "job" for
which she is interviewing in class but any other job she wants once she
leaves the university.

My feet drag just thinking about her, not in anger but in sadness
that the reality of life is that it just isn't so. We have worked for weeks now
with these women, helping them not only to recognize and identify their
abilities but to prepare to sell these unique abilities to potential employ-
ers. We have helped them experience and express their personal power,
but now, at this crucial juncture of classroom and world, we must help
them make the fragile connection between that power and the reality
called accommodation.

"You've got to be kidding!"

I am telling a friend about this chapter, and her voice rises to
near-scream pitch. She asks how, after working with women all these
years, I can now suggest that they accommodate.

"Women have been accommodating for a million years, " she
said. "I can't believe you're asking that we do it again."

There are two important points that my friend has overlooked:
(1) Accommodation is a fact of life, and (2) accommodation is an idea
that is new to many women.

Accommodation as a Fact of Life

There is nothing I would like better than to be able, as a result of what we
have learned over the past few decades, to be the bearer of the news to
the world that each of us is at last free to do whatever we please. I wish I

could tell all the women in my classes and whom I counsel and speak to that there is now a world out there waiting for each of us and our unique talents, bare feet and all. I wish I could say that I've seen evidence that marriages can thrive, friendships can bloom, and love can flourish in an atmosphere in which chips are firmly attached to shoulders, heels are dug in the ground, and positions are staked out and defended. But I can't. How good it would be if we could say that we have moved from the dark night of self-denial into a sunlit time in which simply being one-self guarantees happiness. But that is not the way it is.

Accommodation is a fact of life, not only of the "life" defined by the decade in which we live, but of the life force itself. As I look out the window over my typewriter, I can see that one of the birch trees on the riverbank has grown diagonally toward the south to avoid being totally shaded by the large oaks and pines. Next to my desk, I watch my cat chew the dried fronds off my palm plant; he cannot get to his favorite outdoor twigs because of the snowdrifts. In my chair, I am aware of my-self watching my cat and allowing him to do this because I want him here with me in this room.

By these moves the birch has not stopped being a birch tree, the cat has not given up his needs, and I have not given in to the cat. Rather, each of us has accommodated to the reality of the world in which we live and the interaction of all the ingredients of that world. When the birch can no longer get enough light, it will die. When the cat begins eating plants I care more about than I do his esteem, he will be banished to his bed. When I decide to do this banishing, I must know that I run the risk of the loss of his company for the rest of the afternoon and evening. These, too, are realities.

Because humans are "obviously" different from birch trees and cats, it becomes tempting for us to uplevel our experiences to the point where they need a whole other set of rules and regulations. But the rules of accomodation flow across kingdoms, phyla, classes, and orders. The partner in a marriage who does not realize that he or she will sometimes have to move out from under the "shade" of the other partner to survive, the friend who does not realize that she or he must sometimes make allowances for you because of your personal "snowdrifts," and the per-son who does not realize the risks as well as the joy in standing one's own ground are partners in relationships that are headed for extinction.

The tricky part for us as humans is that it is not always apparent in relationships just who is the birch and who the pine, who the cat and who the owner. It is also not apparent—although there are those who are ready to line up and cheer for both sides—which is the better in these pairs. Fortunately, because we are human and because we have human capabilities, we do not have to decide which of these we will be: sometimes we can be the pine, sometimes the birch, sometimes the cat, and sometimes the owner. But being human, we also have the responsibility to make that choice on the basis of each situation in which we find ourselves. That's what accommodation is all about.

Beyond Settling to Accommodation

"How can you talk about personal power for women in one breath and accommodation in the next?" a student asked me one day. "Now that I feel strong, I'll be darned if I'm going to 'accommodate' anyone."

Except that she is going to have to because accommodation, as I have written above, is a fact of life. The reason that I "talk about personal power in one breath and accommodation in the next" is that the first is so necessary if we are to live with the reality of the second. Without a sense of personal power and self-esteem we simply cannot face the reality of accommodation in the human experience, and in fleeing from that reality, we flee from life itself.

When my friend says that women have accommodated for "a million years" she is mistaken. It has only been in recent years that women in large numbers have developed the personal strength necessary to accommodate. Many still have not reached that point. What women were doing—and what many still are—may have looked like accommodation but is, in fact, the devitalized behavior known as "settling." In settling we act like the birch tree that, not realizing the reality of life, refuses to adapt, gets smothered by pines, withers, and dies. Other times we act like the cat who settles for the fact that she can't go outside to play where and when she wants and goes to pout and get fat in the corner. Then, attempting to compensate for the bad feelings produced by settling, we may try to force our way up through the pines or chew up all the plants in sight and then, as we survey the wreckage, wonder where it all went wrong. Or we may become like the owner who screams angrily at the cat for acting out its catness, and then wonder why we are left all alone.

It is only now that women are beginning to see that without accommodation there can be no talk of either inner peace or peace in the world. We are beginning to see that without accommodation all of our energy goes into simply surviving. We are beginning, finally, to understand that the beautiful way of life called accommodation not only does not "put us down" but actually carries us along in the flow of life if we use it wisely.

Accommodation as Decision

The primary difference between settling and accommodation is decision. Accommodation not preceded by decision making is just settling with a fancier name. Just as we cannot face the reality of the need for accommodation without a sense of self-esteem, neither can we decide how and when we are going to accommodate without a sense of personal strength.

Accommodation is not a security blanket to be wrapped around ourselves before we sally forth into the world with a simpering smile on our faces and a flower clutched in our hand. Even the birch that struggles toward the sun is no wimp; at its core it knows the score.

As you grow in strength you find that there are many times when your decision-making process will bring you to the point of accommodation: you will decide that you will wait dinner for someone or wait for a client who is late or listen to a roommate's complaints one more time or forgive the dentist for filling the wrong tooth. But accommodation can only be practiced if you can genuinely say, "This just doesn't matter that much" or "It matters but there is something else here that matters more"—my time, my health, the relationship. If you decide that the situation does matter to you and that you need to take a stand, you will not be able to live with any integrity unless you do. In these cases, you will not be willing to accommodate.

In the times when I have not been willing to accommodate I have sent back dinners to restaurant kitchens as many as three times because they were not done right, and I have had painters redo rooms for the same reason. I have marched in the cold of a Wisconsin winter for something I believed in and been dumped into a Colorado lake because I wouldn't accommodate on another. I was sometimes the "only" mother who would not give in and let her child attend a party to which "everyone" was going, and there have been times I have been unwilling or unable to spend the time a friendship required and have had to face the fact that I was the cause of its ending.

Accommodation as Conflict Management

For some of us, maturing into our strength means that the decision to accommodate comes not so much because of the life event itself but with the sheer realization that to hassle about it further is just not worth the time and energy it will take. Each of us, later or sooner, comes to the realization that as humans we have just so much time on this earth and just so much energy to expend. When they are gone, they are gone. Deciding which things are worth standing firm on, and then letting go of the rest, can provide us with stores of energy and time to use for more creative pursuits.

My own realization of the positive uses of accommodation came most vividly through a reevaluation of my own marriage after a period of discord. Fresh from a long period of self-growth on my part, I was dismayed to find that it had not been paralleled on my husband's. Although I knew intellectually—and taught!—that one part of a family system cannot change without conferring change upon all others, emotionally I did not want to accept the fact that the changer (me) cannot determine what that conferred change will be. In other words, the changes I had made in my life, while totally positive for me, were not one hundred percent positive for our relationship because they did not take into account that another person was involved. When my attempts at "open, honest communication" sometimes escalated into shouting matches, I knew it was time to consider alternatives. Using my own Reality Probe, I came up with the following: (1) I love my husband and want to stay in the marriage, (2) I do not like chronic conflict, (3) I am an intuitive communicator, strong and sometimes stubborn, (4) my husband is a pragmatic noncommunicator, strong and always stubborn, and (5) if I want something to change I have to be willing to define it, decide what I am going to do about it, and begin.

As I reviewed the situation I began to see that my attempts to negotiate conflict (a process that demands high-level communication skills) with a noncommunicator was a no-win situation. I also knew that the avoidance that I had begun to use is an inauthentic response to a vital relationship such as ours and that the conflict strategies of attack or retreat are, from my point of view, totally nonproductive. I decided to build on our shared love and respect for each other by the appropriate use of accommodation. I was not willing to negate myself by swallowing my thoughts and words in the interest of accommodation, but I was willing to stop insisting that I share each and every one of them with him. Instead, I began to find other places in which to express them: over lunch with a friend, in my journal, in graduate school, with my students. I made the conscious decision to affirm each of us: our strengths (his integrity of thought and action and his marvelous solidity; my ability to carry through and make things happen and my spirit-which-won't-sit-still), our weaknesses (pick a number), our capacity for having fun together, and our right to live together not only in harmony but in joy.

I also began the conscious attempt to let things go which I once would have felt had to be argued to their knees, and in the process I found out how few of them really matter that much. At first it felt strange, but it was not long before this was the only way I wanted to be. My husband's response was not only willing but enthusiastic.

As I began a more conscious effort to share the "miracle" of accommodation with my students, clients, and friends, I saw time and again how well it worked. Marianne's experience is typical:

At 25, Marianne is married to a bank manager ten years her senior who, by her description, "pulled himself up out of a really tacky family to become someone." Her dislike for their "tackiness" caused her to devise a strategy of "clamming up" whenever she and her husband would visit his family. Since they lived less than thirty miles away, the visits came often. Whenever the family would try to encourage her to join in their apparently lively discussions, Marianne would sit back in silence, pick up a magazine, or even go out and sit in the car. She said that even when she felt like talking she would keep quiet "to show them how dumb they are." As a result of her actions, she and her husband always had a fight in the car on the way home. In the wake of these fights, the "air would be tense" around the house for a couple of days afterward.

Marianne's concerns had surfaced in class, and as we talked later, she said that she loved her husband and wanted to stay in the marriage. She said the "in-law problem" was the only thing getting in the way of what she considered "a pretty decent life."

I asked Marianne to try an experiment in accommodation, which she initially refused. A week later she came back and agreed to try it. I asked her to note very intentionally, on the next visit to the family, every event of the day. I asked her to pause before each and decide whether it was worth spending energy on either as she sat there or later, in the car. Where possible, I asked her to "go with the flow" and let the conversation simply go by.

When she came back to see me the next week she said she was surprised to find that there were only two things that really bothered her: the family's assumption that they would all spend Thanksgiving together and her sister-in-law's insistence upon holding Marianne's 16-month-old baby during the entire visit. She was able, Marianne said, to let most of the other things take place without getting involved, but these "really made me mad." I helped her see how she could stand firm on these two issues without carrying around a chronic grudge against the entire family. I suggested that before her next visit she allow herself to "lighten up" even when the conversations got as "dumb" as she described them to be. I encouraged her to enter into the conversations from time to time if it was not too uncomfortable for her.

A month later Marianne reported feeling "lighter" and "freer" than she ever had before after a family visit. She had told them that she and her husband and son had made other plans for Thanksgiving and they had been disappointed yet agreeable, and she had been able, in what she called "a mildly decent way," to extricate her son from his aunt's clutches.

"I just sort of let things happen," she said. "I realized that the world wasn't going to come to an end just because these jokers hadn't seen the latest Bergman film or if my husband's father called his wife 'ma.' I've got to admit there's a lot of love in that family, and as I sat there I began to feel it for the first time."

Accommodation as Meditation

For many of us, the use of daily meditation practice has been of tremendous help in being able to sort out what is worth fighting for and what we can let go. As we learn to let go of our thoughts on a regular basis during our daily practice, we find that it is easier to let go of some of the "stuff" that keeps us stuck in the past or living in the future. We are able to let go of many of the things we once thought we had to argue to completion but which we now see have been eating away our lives.

At a management seminar I met Carola, 41, and as the conversation turned to ways we had found helpful in the living of our lives, she told me of how daily contemplative time had helped her in some of her relationships. She described a recent visit to California to see her father this way:

"We are still poles apart in our beliefs and yet I do love and affirm him. Suddenly I'm willing to let it go at that. I know that he loves me in his own way, but since affirming is not part of that way, I can't expect it and I'm going to stop knocking myself out to 'make it happen.' Many of our conversations could be just as upsetting to me now as they used to be, but they aren't because I just let them float by. I am as loving to him as possible, but it doesn't feel phony because for the first time in my life I *do* feel loving toward him. I love him for who he is, not who I always wanted him to be. I'm a big girl now. It feels like it's past time to keep whining about what might have been and start enjoying what is."

A woman who began daily meditation in one of my classes told me recently that she has a new relationship with her 14-year-old-son:

"I used to nag him from morning to night about his schoolwork. He wants to get into Brown for pre-med, and I knew that if he so much as brought home an A minus it was all over. Then last October one of the boys in his class was killed in a head-on collision. After the funeral I kept looking at my son and thinking 'It could have been him.' I started thinking that if it had been, our last conversation was me shouting at the front door about his homework. It dawned on me that we hadn't talked about anything else in months. Did I really want to sacrifice the years I had with him like this? Meditation has helped a lot. At first I'd just sit there and my mind would go over lists of things I had to do that day. I thought that was great—like I was fooling someone—but finally I woke up to the fact that it was just another form of 'futuring.' I've gotten now to where I can just sit and empty my mind and let myself be in the moment. I think it's the first time I've done that since I was a little kid."

Meditation is not a mysterious ritual or a pop psychology piece that can be whipped out now and then when the going gets tough. Meditation is a time in which we can connect or reconnect body, mind, and soul with the eternal and which can be incorporated into everyday life as easily as any other activity that we feel is important. The only three things that are absolutely necessary to begin are a quiet place where you will be undisturbed for at least fifteen minutes, a comfortable position, and a quiet, empty mind.

The reasons people give for not being able to include meditation in their lives are many, but the most frequently given are that they cannot find the time or space to do it or that they do not have the patience or the know-how to carry it out.

1. "I don't have time."

"Meditation? The only 'meditation' I have time for is when I get in bed and go to sleep."

This is the reaction I often get from women who work outside their homes as well as from full-time homemakers with young children. Usually it is not until these women either have experienced the benefits of daily meditation in one of my classes or have been brought by life to a crisis point that they are willing to look at the fact that scheduling fifteen minutes a day to meditate takes little more effort than scheduling twice-a-day toothbrushing and not as much as getting to swim lessons.

There is no "right" time to meditate, but once you have selected a time for yourself, you need to claim that time as yours, taking it as seriously as you would a child's music lesson or a husband's appointment at the racquetball court. You must be willing to ignore others who dismiss the importance of your "just sitting" or laugh at the "foolishness" of it.

I am not a "morning person," but I have found that, for me, an hour of body movement and meditation practice each morning sets the tone for my entire day. The very act of shutting the door to the room in which I meditate and *letting the world go on without me* is a powerful reinforcement of the fact that, indeed, the world can and does go on without me all the time and that I need not, therefore, be overly concerned with holding it up! My own schedule is one that includes not only my responsibilities at the university but a great deal of travel, consulting, speaking, and writing, in addition to the time I want to spend with my family. People often ask how I can "fit" meditation into such a schedule. The reality is that it is meditation that makes such a schedule possible for me. In starting each day—whether at home or on the road—with the centering that meditation provides, I am more able to handle what that day will bring without fragmentation.

At the time you have decided upon, go into the place you have chosen to meditate, shut the door, sit down in a comfortable position, and begin. Barring fire or similar emergency, let the rest of the world go by.

2. "I can't find space to be alone."

If you can find space alone in which to take a shower or a bath, you can find space alone to meditate! (If you are the mother of young children who says you cannot find space to take a bath alone, then you must immediately move to correct this situation by trading time with your husband or a friend or by hiring a sitter, if only for a half hour. A human being who does not have some alone time each day will not survive long without becoming ill.) If the bathroom is honestly the only place you can meditate, use it, but in the interest of comfort it is preferable to choose another room. Some of us have the luxury of our own "quiet room," but if you don't, claim a bedroom, den, or living room as your own for a small part of each day. I prefer the connectedness to earth and sky that is provided by a cross-legged position on the floor. If you are comfortable in that position, on a zafu or a pillow, use it. If not, sit on a chair, a couch, or the corner of your bed. Do not become so caught up in "doing it right" that you prevent yourself from experiencing this chance to deepen and strengthen your sense of wholeness. If it is quiet and you are comfortable enough not to be aware of your body, you are doing it right.

I have taught meditation practice to women in nursing homes who are unable to move from wheelchairs. Do not use age or disability as an excuse not to meditate.

3. "I don't have the patience."

Most of us, being human, are impatient folk. Most of us come to our meditation impatiently. The beauty of the process is that it teaches us patience by requiring of us that we do nothing more at first than *sit and let it be.*

Once you are seated in a comfortable, quiet place, become aware only of your breathing. Let any thoughts that come into your mind float on by as if they were birds or clouds. Do not attempt to push them out of the way; let them pass. Breathe in and breathe out normally and naturally. The secret of emptying your mind is not to follow up on the thoughts that come into it. Any thought that is not followed up on is a thought that will disappear of its own accord, without force or action on your part.

During the first days or weeks that you attempt this form of meditation you may find that "it doesn't work." You will become frustrated because "nothing happens." That is exactly the point! Slowly, gradually, and *in its own time,* the practice of meditation will teach you on deep levels of your being how to let things go without that first flash of emotion that clouds your decision-making process. Slowly but irrevocably, you will find this transferring itself into the other parts of your daily life.

4. "I don't understand how to meditate."

The steps above are the basis for meditation practice. For some, they are enough. Many of us incorporate our own spiritual beliefs or our own religious practice into our meditation. Some of us use a form of meditation in which we combine mind-emptying with receptive prayer and the contemplation of scripture. Some people may want to find a book that describes meditation practice; a good choice is Lawrence LeShan's *How to Meditate.* Still others may want to look for a retreat center where they can begin their meditation practice along with others in a more structured way. These are decisions each person will make on her own as she moves more deeply into her commitment to meditation.

Those of us for whom meditation has become a way of life find it hard to explain fully the benefits that have come to us from this practice. We are hesitant, I think, because we do not want this to be interpreted as yet another in the endless series of "how-to's." Quite the opposite, meditation is not a crutch to be used until you get "better" or to get you through the hard times. It is a way of life that both centers you in your own being and connects you with the flow of all life in a way that makes accommodation not only possible but natural. As with accommodation, the way of meditation winds back to antiquity, yet it is as new as tomorrow's dawn for those who have not yet discovered its power.

Accommodation as Reconciliation

We are sitting in my living room. She is an old friend I have not seen in five years, and in that time she has divorced her husband. Her anger is still very close to the surface: she still hates him, she says, for having destroyed their lives with this anger. Now she brings out her journal and asks me to read it.

"If only he would leave, die, have an affair, get on with his own life," she has written. "But he seems stuck in some awful rut that he both despises and yet holds onto. A desperate protection. It reminds me of my old 'familiar pain.' Where is the aliveness that was there when I married this man? What combination, ratio, sum of tiny miserable abrasions wore him down to this huge, gaping pain that won't heal? Sex seemed at one time to ease the pain, to help with the healing, to put some sort of benediction on our being together. But it no longer helps and it feels like a worse-than-rape. It feels degrading because it is dead. The degradation fills the rest of our lives. His anger covers both of us like rose spray dust seeping into our pores and our lives. His anger has in it all the depression and sadness and fear he has ever felt at the hands of all the others in his life who didn't love him and appreciate him. Poor sick man. Boy. And all these years I felt that I was the one that was weak, with the periods that wouldn't stay put and the crying that wouldn't stop."

I want to run from the room. I feel too weary to confront her with the reality of her own self-inflicted pain because she is a friend, not a client, and I know that confrontation demands the picking up of pieces best done in a more professional setting than the one in which we find ourselves.

But in the course of our long conversation before the fireplace in my living room that night I did finally ask her if she realized that she had escaped the "rose dust" of her husband's anger only to lose herself in the poisonous fog of her own.

She had made the decision not to accommodate within her marriage any longer: she had divorced him. But then she had, in effect, kept herself imprisoned by her own anger, giving him the same hold over her that he had had during the final years of their marriage. She had never done the anger and grief work demanded by the divorce and the pain that had gone before, and therefore she was not ready to attempt accommodation. For my friend and for so many others, the opportunity—and the desire—to forgive personally the ex-husband/lover/roommate who hurt them is long gone. But forgiveness must take place *within them* or their healing will never be complete.

To attempt to forgive prematurely is a pseudo-accommodation, and it is dangerous. It can plunge you into depression or it can take you into a chronic belligerence toward life which shows up in your need to take over others' lives or to gossip and put down others. It can, because it is still full of unexpressed anger, stain the fabric of your life to the point where everything you see and do is colored by the taint of the hatred.

What is needed instead is time to sort through the anger, naming it, discussing it, and then discarding it. If possible, do this in the company of a trained professional who will give you the time you need but will also encourage you finally to bring the matter to closure, forgive the other and yourself, and get on with your life. Bosses fire us despite our best efforts, lovers leave, children don't live up to our expectations, friends turn their backs on us, and business partners stab them. Life provides daily chances for anger to bubble up around us and engulf us in its brine. If we choose to live our lives in that foment, we have that choice but we need, also, to know that there is another, better choice.

The forgiveness of which I write is not the cheery dismissal of the very real pain that took place in our lives. It is not the false forgiveness that is out of the mouth but stuck deep in the gut. It is, instead, a forgiveness based on the knowledge that on this earth we are bound inextricably with other imperfect human beings and that in the nature of things there will be times in which that interaction will bring us pain. It is forgiveness that stems from the knowledge that our own time is limited and that it, and we, are worth more than to serve as a receptacle for hate.

Some of the women who have taken time to forgive themselves and the person who has hurt them have told me that they, like Marianne, feel lighter and freer. "It's as if," one woman said, "I am moving *with* life instead of against it."

Reconciliation is often thought to mean only the reunion of two people who have been estranged. It is that, but it can also be much more. Even when you are out of physical and psychic touch with the person who has hurt you deeply, you can participate in reconciliation. For the act of reconciliation can be a marvelous time of accommodation to oneself, a time in which you can forgive yourself, make peace with yourself, give yourself credit for what you did accomplish within a relationship, a time in which you can accept yourself as a person of value despite what has happened. It can be a time in which the parts of yourself that hurt so much are allowed to heal—gathered together in communion.

It can be the time in which you allow the harmony of yourself to be restored.

8

Race to Nowhere, Journey to Everywhere

"If I Just Run a Little Faster, I'll Catch Up"

It is a lazy Sunday morning, a delicious rare time in which you can loll in bed, sip endless cups of coffee, burrow into the bag of almond croissants that you bought even though you're still trying to get rid of six pounds. You stretch and think about the day. Maybe a long soak in the avocado bath oil to start, maybe later a run. Forget the work you brought home from the office or the stuff you didn't finish around the house this week. Your kids are gone for the day, your husband is out of town, or for whatever reason the day is yours. The sun is shining, and you feel fantastic. You pour yourself some more coffee, pick up the Sunday paper, and snuggle into the pillows to read it.

A mistake.

Within minutes you find out that the color you chose for your new carpet, which will be laid on Tuesday, is obsolete. Ditto your new suit, which itself has become anachronistic. The idea you'd planned to present at the office next week has been called by an analyst interviewed on page 2 of the business section "hopelessly byzantine," and a psychologist makes it abundantly clear that your decision to stop breastfeeding your baby at eight months will have lifetime implications for your entire family. By the time you have finished the medical column you have serious doubts whether your doctor really does know anything about endometriosis. And there, where you least expected to find her, is a picture of an old classmate of yours who has just won a Woman of the Year award for her outstanding achievements as a business owner, wife, mother of four *cum laude* children, board member, and volunteer for a half-dozen groups. And she looks fantastic.

Your croissant turns to sawdust in your mouth. The coffee is not only cold but bitter. You toss the paper down. Around you everyone else in the world is achieving. Having tossed out their tailored blazers and banished the "boring" earth tones from their living rooms and carved out quality time for the grandchildren and a world cruise, other women are marching ahead with renewed purpose while you lie abed, stacks of work undone around you, staring at an empty orange juice glass. The sun, coming through the window, falls directly on the layer of dust on your bedside table.

"Everyone Else Has It All Together, and Their Packaging Is Better"

In a darkened classroom, I sit with a group of women as they explain the slides they have drawn to typify themselves. Maureen is speaking as her slide, which depicts a dour-looking face against a blank background, is projected against the wall:

"My eyes are to one side in the drawing because I am always looking around to see who is catching up with me and what others are doing. I am always looking around to see how I am doing in comparison to others."

There is an audible gasp from the other women in the room. Maureen is a beautiful woman, tall and slim, with silky black hair and olive skin. She is a nurse. She is married to a professional man and they have two children. She is clearly considered by the group to be one of its outstanding members; if a sociogram were to be made of the class, I predict that many paths would lead to her. But now she has admitted to the others her feelings of inadequacy, and they are busy readjusting their thinking. If Maureen, who "obviously" does not have to worry about money, job, children, husband, looks, or health, feels this insecure, where, each of them asks herself, does that leave me?

In all the years I've worked with women I have seen absolutely no correlation between the way a woman looks or the house she lives in or the number of other "good" things she has in her life and how she feels about herself. Yet the belief in this correlation remains so strong and pervasive that we often become driven by it to spending our lives searching for the "goodies" that will deliver our own happy ending. As I listened to Maureen I was reminded of a woman I once knew in Wyoming, a large, beautiful woman with clear ivory skin who was widely admired for her looks and the parties she gave. But she thought she was ugly and overweight, and for all the years I knew her she was on a diet. She was not on a diet that is an awareness that certain foods cause certain reactions in her body, but a diet that demanded daily guilt-tripping before and after each meal. It was no fun to have lunch with her, nor is it with anyone else who precedes the giving of the order, the first bite, and every subsequent bite with the disclaimer "I shouldn't." How much more enjoyable it could be for these women if they would pull out all the stops for the honest and wildly orgasmic pleasure of a piece of cheesecake slathered with wild blueberries from time to time rather than confuse their digestive juices with the mixed messages of the half-enjoyed mousse. How much more enjoyable to celebrate the beauty of a *zaftig* body by pulling out all the stops and dressing it in clothes and colors you enjoy than to hide behind someone else's idea of a slimming fashion which is neither slimming (why would you want to slim a beautiful body like that?) nor fashionable.

I am reminded also of some of the other women assumed to have had it all together:

- Jane, a bright, wonderfully attractive student of mine, wife of the president of a small manufacturing company, whose house was considered a showplace yet who was quite literally a prisoner in it because of her agoraphobia.

- Laurie, an articulate, attractive 27-year-old who, with her husband, graduated from divinity school but thinks of herself as a "loser" because she feels she is not as attractive or as articulate as her husband.

- Frances, 45, whose husband just gave her diamond earrings for the twenty-fifth anniversary of what everyone who knows them considers the "perfect marriage," yet who says she cannot remember the last time she felt happy.

- Karen, a music teacher with a phenomenal soprano voice who thought because her husband had left her that she was "a bag of trash" and went methodically about the business of seeing to it that she looked as much like one as possible.

- Sheree, 53, who dropped out of her ballet class, striking silver-gray hair, talent, and all, because everyone else in the class was so much younger.

As women have described their feelings of inadequacy to me over the years I have often asked them why they haven't shared them with their friends, members of their clubs, or their church circles. They have stared at me in disbelief that I would ask such a question, and their answers have been identical: "I wouldn't dare admit it. Everyone else has it all together."

The belief that others have it all together can make us pick so endlessly at the wrapping of our own package that we have no time to enjoy the gift it contains: us! Who among us cannot immediately access from our memory the envy we felt at the sight of another woman's waist-length hair, merit raise, figure in a bikini, white terrazzo bathroom, tennis serve, rose garden, sales contract, or the food she served for —— (fill in the blank). And who among us does not recall the endless strategies we've devised to remedy the deficiencies in ourselves so that we could attain one or more of the "goodies" which made these others so special?

I remember the hours I pored over *Seventeen* magazine when I was that age, wondering how I could achieve anything near the Lana Turner looks of that little blonde in our senior class who, with one look from her *Postman Always Rings Twice* eyes, could have the guys falling off their chairs. In college those of us with full wardrobes of cashmere sweaters were assumed to have the package pretty well tied up, but by the 1960s some of us were falling behind again, and it was the woman who had actually managed a home with wall-to-wall carpeting in every room, both baths-and-a-half, and the furnace room who was the standard for comparison. If you didn't look good braless you were, quite literally, a bust in the 1970s, and the standard for having it all together as the decade ended became the ability to balance job and family with aplomb and to tell boss, husband, and world to go to hell without missing a beat.

Jobs, men, looks, lives—we've used them all to compute whether or not others have it all together. Never in history, though, has there been a time such as the one in which we now live in which communications have made it so possible for us to become aware of our presumed insufficiencies. Where once a woman had to leave her small town to find out how "out of it" she was, today a dozen evidences of it come into our homes each evening on the news and every morning on the talk shows. Where once it might have been suggested to us by our doctor or a fashion magazine that we might want to lose a few pounds, today we are beaten over the head with the reminder that not to be thin is to be invisible. As you relax in the hot tub you have finally been able to afford, you realize that it is yesterday's news and that the rest of the world is rushing to the simplicity of the log cabin again. Even a decade ago a woman could look around her neighborhood or her office and see other women just "there," but today we can scarcely go to the mailbox or the water cooler without hearing of yet another seminar that promises to bring all of our abilities and complexion colors into such a rainbow of harmony that our happy ending is assured. All we have to do, of course, is find time for it on our calendar and money for it in our budget—and finish it before it goes out of style—and the pot of gold is ours.

I've always felt that one of the neatest things done by medicine is that little lecture that is supposedly given prior to all cosmetic surgeries about the fact that the surgery will not automatically make a rotten life blessed or a previously nonexistent self-esteem spring to life in the recovery room. I was in on the celebration when a friend unveiled her new nose. I know that droopy facial and body parts can be a daily lesson in gravity that many women can do without and that nonexistent body parts can be anything from an annoyance to a heartbreak. But I've also known enough beautiful, unhappy women who've spent years looking over their shoulders to see who is catching up to know the truth in the surgeons' words.

Rewrapping one's personal package can be just the right thing for you to do. Improving your mind, your voice, your body, your home can enhance your life tremendously. But doing it carries with it, also, the potential for depression if the expectations you place upon the improvement are beyond what the improvement itself can deliver. How you feel about the improvement will, in almost every case, depend upon the reasons you had for undertaking it. As a statement of who you already are, as something you will enjoy, to improve your health, for the sheer fun of doing it—it makes sense. But if you are rewrapping parts of your life out of the mistaken belief that once the new ribbons are tied in place you will walk off ahead of the pack into your personal sunset, never again to be bothered by fear, doubt, or things that go bump in the night, you are in for severe disappointment.

Until you are enough, all the new packaging in the world will never be enough. When finally you realize that you *are* enough and that packaging rarely determines content, you are free to use and enjoy as much or as little of it as you choose.

The most valuable benefit of support groups has been their ability to cut through the notion that each of us is alone in our insecurities about ourselves and our relationship with others. The reality is that we are all far more alike than we are different. Our problems and our fears are uniquely and painfully ours, but they are also ones that, with only slight modifications, are the problems and pains of millions of other human beings. Once we realize this and believe it, we can begin to accept our own deficiencies and honor our own strengths because we know that they are just the deficiencies and strengths of others in a slightly different configuration! The more we allow ourselves to be open to others and the more we really listen to what they have to say, the more we will realize that nothing human is perfect, no human being "has it all to-gether," and at some time or another each of us ends up scrambling for the cellophane tape.

"If I Just Try Harder, I'll Make It"

I cannot begin to guess how many women's letters and conversations with me have begun like this one: "Fear and lack of self-confidence have plagued me throughout my life, and yet I know there are many things I would still like to do. It's just that I look around and *see how well every-one else does things,* and I know if I tried them I'd probably fail." [Italics added.]

Fear of not measuring up to others also plagues most of the Women Helping Women classes we teach. In one Albuquerque class, as I met with five of the trainees for their weekly conferences, each wom-an's main concern was that she was not doing as well as the others in the class.

Dusty, a lovely, lively 35-year-old mother of two, called me sev-eral times after being accepted into a WHW class to say she wasn't going to attend because she knew she couldn't handle all the work. Like so many of the other returning students, Dusty was frightened by the thought of being in school again after so many years away from the dis-cipline required by daily study. Sensing that she wanted to attend and knowing from her interview materials that she could do the work, I urged her to come the first day just to meet the class. She came, but by noon she had disappeared. When I phoned her home I found that she had been so dismayed by "how smart everyone else in class was" (although none had said much more than her name and where she was from) that she had simply given up before she'd begun. I urged her back once more and, with continued encouragement, she stayed on to finish the class successfully. More important, after working with the other women in her class she began to understand, she said, that no matter how "to-gether" others appear to be on the surface, they are often feeling pretty much the way we are at any given moment in time.

For so many years women have been afraid to try. If they did try, it was the passive "trying" epitomized by the 55-year-old woman who recently told me she is still "trying to please others." Then, as women began to move out into new endeavors, they often, like Dusty, became intimidated when others appeared to be stronger, more confident, or "better" than they. Abby, for example, had never finished high school and so, despite her tremendous ability as a group leader and organizer, lacked the personal confidence to seek further education. LeeAnn, a talented writer and researcher, tells me she is afraid to let "herself" show because her colleagues might not consider her "professional." Teri, a gifted pianist, came in second in a Liszt contest and was so intimidated by her "failure" that she has rarely played the piano since.

Much of our work in Women Helping Women has been based on providing an environment in which women can try—their skills, their abilities, and their selves—in an atmosphere in which one misstep is not a lifetime stigma. Women who have never been able to speak in front of a group before reach the point where they can address whole rooms full of people. Women who haven't done a "theme" in thirty years surprise themselves by turning in excellent term papers, and women near paralysis from test anxiety learn how to relax and write to successful completion. Women who have never worked outside their homes find jobs they had only dreamed possible, and others use newfound skills in interpersonal relations and self-selling to move from routine jobs to meaningful ones. Women who have never asked their gynecologist or auto mechanic a question are now able to, and women who had thought they were too old to exercise or meditate or look good, find they can.

But as I travel throughout the country I am beginning to see some disconcerting signs that, once again, the new "answer" has turned back on itself and becomes the old question: When did enough become too much? When did trying stop being a positive reaching out and start being a relentless imperative that keeps women striving in every part and moment of their lives?

Increasingly I see women who do not seem to realize that trying, like all of life, consists of ebb and flow. Passive for so long, they have moved into a time of successful activity, and now, almost like overrevved motors, they seem unable to wind down. Even when they are exhausted, even when the thing they are doing is supposed to be for pleasure, even when what they are experiencing is beyond human control, the trying goes on.

- A 38-year-old housewife tells me she is "still trying" to get her body in shape and is enrolled in four different exercise classes, "one for each part of my body." When I ask her if she enjoys any of this, she looks at me as if I'm speaking another language.

- An associate professor in her late fifties with severe arthritis tells me that she is exhausted from administering four federal grants, teaching a full load, and taking care of an invalid mother, but has applied for a fifth grant so that "my department chair will sit up and take notice."

- A woman whose cancer has metastasized is bitter, not only about the spread of the disease but because she had used healing imagery and it hasn't worked. "Maybe," she said, "I just didn't try hard enough."

- A friend tells me that she is so unhappy because of the breakup of a relationship that seemed "meant to be" that she is going to try one more time to reach out to him.

- A student who says she has been "trying" to meditate for six months says she is going to take a seminar on meditation this summer so she can "get it right."

In the tension within each of their voices I hear the injunction they are giving themselves: If I just try harder I'll make it.

When any of us look to others for appreciation of who we are and what we've accomplished, we set ourselves up for disappointment. For any number of reasons—they don't see, they don't care, they don't know how to express it, they don't take time to express it—others don't always come through, and we can go a lifetime without getting the appreciation we think we deserve. As women, we have begun to learn we must give ourselves the appreciation and affirmation we seek. But to give yourself appreciation, you have to review your performance, and in turning over that task to yourself, you may have unwittingly saddled yourself with the world's toughest taskmaster. Unless you have become strong enough to be gentle with yourself, you can be so hard on yourself that no performance, no matter how good, is good enough. As for the less-than-good performances, they can take you down into an abyss of despair and self-loathing. The only answer, you decide, is to try harder. You set for yourself a schedule of perfection that leaves no moment unaccounted for and no worthy cause unattended. If you are in the helping profession, or a parent, you veer dangerously close to a messiah complex. If you are a business person you stake out the world as your hunting grounds. When you fall short you berate yourself and vow to try harder next time. Everyone else is doing it and so can you.

The bad news and good news about all this is that everyone is not doing it and you can't either. Examples:

- It is now a given that daily exercise and certain eating habits are important in keeping the body working effectively. But having fun is also one of life's necessities. When all of your spare time is spent trying harder and harder to look good and to be healthy, you run the risk of ending up with no time to enjoy that body that looks and feels so good.

- High-quality research is respected within academic circles and may earn attention for us as researchers. But adding one more task to an already overburdened mind and body to assure that others will "sit up and take notice" may mean that the sitting up and noticing may take place at your hospital bedside or at your funeral.

- The use of healing imagery has been highly beneficial to many cancer patients and people with other diseases. But the reality remains that no matter how much we do, we can only do what is *humanly* possible. No matter how well we care for our health, the fact remains that we still sicken and we still die. How hard we try to stay well is not always a measure of whether or not we will succeed; we simply do not have all of the answers. Rather than using the very positive new/old healing methods as sticks with which to beat ourselves into "wellness," it is much more effective to cooperate with them in allowing them to work in their own

time and their own ways and to accept the fact that, despite
our best efforts, we do not always get what we think we want.

- Despite the pain that threatens to overwhelm us and the
  feeling that we cannot go on without him, despite our very
  best efforts and our deepest love, we can and do lose our
  husbands and lovers through breakups, divorce, and death.
  It makes no sense to add to the existing pain of loss by an
  endless pawing through the "If onlys . . ." Unless you have
  some definite and irrefutable evidence of specific neglect on
  your part, the fact is that you can seldom, through trying
  harder, control the course of another's life or death or of a
  relationship. To assume otherwise is to presume more
  power than you have as a human being.

- "Trying" to meditate is a contradiction in terms since the
  very act of meditation asks that we stop trying and trust, stop
  doing and be. As "meditation workshops" and "wholeness
  weekends" proliferate, we can so abuse the content that it
  becomes just another in a series of hurdles to jump
  "correctly."

As the hurdles we are encouraged to jump become fixtures on
our daily landscape, as they become higher and more widely broadcast,
we are provided with an increasing number of chances to fall back to try
"just one more time" for that final push to perfection. But what would
happen if, just once, we turned back and kept on going? What if, just
once, we let the opportunity slip by or the night unfold without leaving
the house? What would happen if we sat so deeply in contemplation that
we actually felt ourselves being led to decision, or if we spent the whole
day wading in the river or laughed out loud when the group leader suggested that if we would follow his suggestions we'd be "young forever"?
What would happen if we accepted the next opportunity that was offered
to us without worrying about whether or not we'd "do it right"? What if
we blurted out "I don't understand" when we didn't or "I made a mistake" when we did? What if we did a really perfect job on something and

no one else saw it, and that was all right, too? What if we forgave ourselves?

"My Calendar, My Enemy"

This year was going to be different. You were not going to get overextended. You were going to "take time to smell the roses." But here come those old familiar feelings again: tightness in the chest, heart skipping a beat now and then, a dull ache in the pit of your stomach, a band around your head about four o'clock every afternoon which threatens to tighten. But most of all the feeling of running, running, running and never being able to catch up. You wake up in the middle of the night thinking of all you have to do, and your spirit limps at the thought. You think of all the things you'd like to be doing but don't have time for. You ask yourself what life is all about, but you fall asleep from sheer exhaustion before you get your answer.

This is input overload. This is being too busy with too many things. This is the way that you said you would never be again, but you can't stop now because if you just run a little faster you'll catch up.

Whether the catching up is with your own work or whether it is catching up with someone out there or making up for lost time, it is a siren song that can lure you on and on until you forget where it was you were going and why it was you started out in the first place. You have only to read the Sunday paper to know you will never catch up because each second of your life someone new is entering the race—fresh, enthusiastic, full of new ideas and energy. You have only to review your life to realize that you are never going to be able to "catch up with your daily work" if you are this tired, and you have only to think about it for a second to realize that "catching up" is not really what it is all about.

There has been much written in recent years about managing one's time and planning one's life, about calling a halt to the craziness of a twenty-hour day and starting to take time for things that are important to you. Charts, graphs, and goal-setting experiences have been developed to help the "busy woman" get her life in order. When I first taught goal setting in the early 1970s, I would celebrate with women when they got their ideas together and their goals articulated, but I always won-

dered why so many of the intentions never got off the paper. Recently I
met one of the women who had attended one of my self-growth groups
twelve years ago. When I asked her what she was doing, she said she
was still a full-time housewife—weaving, reading, and enjoying her life
immensely. I asked her why she had struggled so mightily, back in the
group, with her goal of finding a teaching job. She admitted that it was
because she thought that was what she "should" be doing.

    I have since come to understand that goals cannot be
achieved—nor should they be attempted—if they are based solely on
that part of ourselves which is concerned with "shoulds" and "oughts"
and what "they" are doing. Such other-directed goals elude us because
they are not congruent with our mind, body, and spirit. A basic rule of
psychology is that unless the input from outside you agrees with how
you feel inside, you will reject it. Since this input is often "good," you may
not reject it outright, but the you-ness of you will reject it in such start-
ingly marvelous ways as making you fall asleep, making you "forget" to
work on what you said you would work on, making you stumble (figura-
tively) as you miss the bus on your way to interview for the job you didn't
really want or (literally) as you fall on the ice on the way to meet the person for dinner you were not really sure you wanted to be with. If you
have allowed your other-directed goals to turn into an entire way of life
for you—a marriage, a divorce, a houseful of children, a fast-track job, a
dull job—its lack of congruence with who you really are may manifest
itself chronically by making you hungry all the time, tired all the time, or
visited periodically by migraines, backaches, or colitis.

    Keepable goals are those made with your entire being, taking
into account the reality, not the fantasy, of your life. It is important to note
that this does not preclude fantasizing about things you might want to
do; it only precludes fantasizing about the present reality of your life. The
decision to find a job, quit a job, start baking bread, stop making Christmas dinner, move in with him, become celibate, have the surgery, get
bifocals, begin yoga, or drive your daughter seventy-five miles to baton
lessons is yours alone to make. Since it is also yours to live with, you
must be prepared to know the difference between reality and fantasy.

    I no longer work with women using conventional goal-setting
exercises. Instead I design, with them, a life-balancing experience based
on each woman's life as it is and each woman's needs, decisions, plans,
fantasies, and dreams as she articulates them. It is only when we give

ourselves permission to take responsibility for looking at our life and deciding how we want to live it, and take responsibility for that decision no
matter how it turns out, that we can even begin to talk about goal setting
as other than a theoretical construct.

The well-lived life has always been a journey rather than a race.
The hectic schedule is more often an excuse for not participating fully in
your life than it is an indication of true productivity on your part.

No matter where you are at this moment, it is not too late for
you to stop the race and get on with your journey, but before you do,
you must be absolutely sure that you want to make this change. You
need to know that if you make this change, your life will never be the
same again. Among other things, you will never again be able to use
"I'm too busy" as an excuse, and you will be opening yourself to the potential for adventures and experiences you are not even aware of at this
moment. You must also sincerely want to change or you will not. Any
ambivalence on your part will reflect itself in your attempts and will sabo-
tage your plans no matter how carefully they are drawn.

Redesigning Your Life

If you were one of my clients who wanted to redesign your life, I would
ask you to come to my office and bring with you your calendar. It would
be best if the calendar had big squares for the days and lots of room for
lists and notes. Contrary to what many people believe, you do not become more tense and "boxed in" when you make lists and organize
your days. Once things are down on lists, marked on calendars, and
planned for, they are out of your head: you are free to enjoy or participate in what you are doing at the moment rather than scrambling to
think of where you should have been or what you should be doing. (If
you are a person whose life demands—as does mine—that she continually create ideas, the very act of putting an upcoming assignment,
speech, lecture, article idea, or agenda on your calendar will plant the
occasion in your unconscious. There you can let it rest and "germinate"
until the time you have scheduled to work on it. When you sit down to
think and write, you will find that much of the preliminary work has been
done by your unconscious, and you are now ready to "harvest the crop"
and get on with your writing and planning. Along the way, of course,

having been aware of the assignment, you have alerted yourself to pick up on any references to it that will be useful to you when you sit down to plan or write.)

After I had talked with you awhile about your life and after I was convinced that you really wanted to move from race to journey, I would turn the job over to the person who can do it best: you. You would be doing your work in ten steps.

1.   *Stop the action.* I would ask you to do this by taking one full day by yourself as a buffer, a time to think and to evaluate. (Take a vacation day from work if necessary, or hire a sitter for your children. You must be alone to think. If you absolutely cannot arrange an entire day, you must have a minimum of four hours alone.) I would ask you to let me know once you have agreed upon the day. Then I would ask you to come back to see me within a week after that day.

Then you would be on your own. When the day you had set aside to think and to work arrived, you would take your calendar, some paper, pencils, and pen and go to the place you have decided to work and complete the remainder of the ten steps.

2.   *Take it in small pieces.* Don't use this time to redo your entire life; if you do, you are bound to fail. Remember, your task is to get out of the race and on with your journey. Look at the next three months on your calendar. Think about them. What do they feel like to you? If you find it hard to breathe when you think about them, you know you were right in planning this change. Begin to take the pieces apart and realign them.

3.   *Look at the month ahead on your calendar.* For the time being, ignore things that are already set, the appointments made and the commitments agreed upon. Now take the rest of the days. Look at those empty spaces that are, at least for the moment, free.

4.   *Call up a feeling of calm and refreshment.* Take a deep breath. Take several more. Get to the calm, deep center of yourself where you really live. Recall and feel a sense of peace and freedom. If you can't do it just by remembering, then imagine yourself at your favorite place: stretched under the sun on the beach as the waves roar in

the distance, lying under the pines in a sun-dappled forest. Relax. Now look at your calendar again. Keeping in touch with your feeling of calm, schedule in at least fifteen minutes a day for meditation (mind-emptying, contemplation, prayer), six days a week, for the next three months. (If you can schedule a half hour, so much the better, but be realistic.) Next, if you do not already exercise on a daily basis, at this time schedule in fifteen to thirty minutes of exercise (walking, dancing, biking, stretching, swimming—your choice), six days a week, for the next three months.

5.   *Do a death trip.* Next, pretend that you are going to die a month from today. What are the things you want to do that you haven't yet done? Remember, next month will be too late: you must do them now or never on this earth. Your choice might be to ride a carousel again, go visit a grandchild, stay in bed all day and order in pizza on the hour, drop out of your car pool, go to Cannes for the film festival, eat all the fudge you really want, try out for a play, enroll in a program leading to a degree, send someone a bouquet of balloons, send yourself a dozen roses, run for public office, call up someone you'd like to get to know and invite her/him to lunch, take a welding course, or study Hebrew. Use the following rules for choice: (a) It must not take up more time than the actual free space you have on your calendar. (b) It must not be damaging to others. (c) It must not cost so much that you back out at the last minute. (Be careful with [c] if you are not used to treating yourself or if you are used to going wild with the checkbook. A good rule here is to estimate the amount you would be willing to pay for a gift for a person you love, and then spend that amount.)

6.   *Write in your want-tos.* All the fantasizing in the world remains in the realm of fantasy if you don't start to move it into the realm of possibility-en-route-to-reality. From among the things that surfaced on your death trip, select one for each of the next three months. Pen them in on your calendar, being very specific about dates and times. If one or more of the things you chose will take more than a month to finish, that's all right, but be sure that you start one during each of the next three months.

7.   *Review existing commitments.* Scan your calendar for the next three months. What things can you jettison? (You must toss out

one old thing for every new thing you add. Since you have now added one new thing for each of the next three months, you must get rid of one thing each month. If you find yourself saying you can't, then you are not ready for this life change.) To help you determine what to toss and what to keep, determine whether the thing is on the calendar because it is *value-intrinsic* (VI) or whether it is there because it has *perceived external value* (PEV). Examples of VI items might be visiting a friend in a nursing home, going for your annual physical, buying groceries, serving on an employee relations committee. VI items are not necessarily fun but they have meaning for you and you "believe" in them. PEV items, on the other hand, are those which make you tired just thinking about them. They don't feed you in any way and, as a result, probably aren't of too much value to others either. These might include attending meetings of organizations in which you have no interest for fear of what others will say if you drop out, eating at the same deli each Thursday even though you hate the food just because a former roommate is the owner, or continuing on with a class in which you have found you have no interest.

8.   *Jettison the PEVs.* Once you have decided, be firm. Not only should you jettison the three PEVs that you need to make way for your "want-tos," but go on from there and get the rest out of your calendar for the next three months. Phone, write, or do what you have to to cancel, but once you have decided, stick to it. Remove them from your calendar. It is important to leave blank spaces on your calendar. These beautiful empty spaces will not only provide you with the literal space you need to balance your activity, but will remind you that it is often in the unscheduled times of our life that we live most fully and authentically.

9.   *Set up the three months on your calendar.* In pen, mark in all appointments that are value-intrinsic, your exercise and meditation times, and the "want-to" for the month. After exercise and meditation have become a part of your life you won't have to write them down, but at the beginning it is important that you do it.

10.   *Make no exceptions.* Short of a real emergency, do not deviate from your plan. The success or failure of this, as of any endeavor, depends upon believing in it enough to stay with it. Be aware

of how quickly PEVs can push their way back onto your calendar and into your life!

I would ask you to phone me once each week for the first month of your new way of living, and then I would ask you to come back to talk with me at the end of that month. At the end of three months, I would talk with you about planning the following three months. At the end of six months, we would have a final meeting as you begin to incorporate life balancing into the years ahead.

If you are like most of us, you will find that the addition to your life of more and more things that feed you and the reduction or omission of things that deplete you will result in a rise in your energy level. You will find that getting things down on lists and out of your head and intentionally leaving empty spaces on your calendar will help you flow with life instead of being led by it. You will also see that by getting out of the race and on with your journey you will begin to interact more freely, creatively, and lovingly toward others.

For so many years women danced to the tunes of others' expectations. We smiled and pleased, curled and tweezed, so that we would be accepted and loved by others. As we became more conscious that reactive behavior is counterproductive to the living of lives, we began to realize that it was important to live out the fullness of our own. But in attempting to do this, many women have only rearranged the words. They have changed the verse from pleasing others to pleasing self, but the same old chorus of shame and guilt for not measuring up remains.

The old song went like this: I am not too bright and not very good-looking. I need someone else to tell me what to do and whether I'm doing it right. If others don't think I'm doing well, they must be right because they are so much smarter than I am. So I'll just hurry up and try harder and then maybe I can please them.

The new words are: I am now a strong, worthwhile person and I live in a world where there are many choices open to me. I can make my own decision about how I'll live. When I look around and see how much I could be doing compared with what I am doing, I can see I'm not measuring up to my potential. If I screw up now, I have only myself to blame. So I'll just try harder and run a little faster and then I'll. . . .

Women have increasingly become tired of living up to everyone else's models of perfection, but we are just beginning to realize that we must get out from the even more exhausting demands of our own. A hurdle is a hurdle is a hurdle, and although we may have moved our locus of control inside ourselves, unrealistic external standards of perfection are just as painful to attempt when we set the crossbar a little higher as when someone else does. It's invigorating to jump until we feel exhilarated, even tired; it is folly to jump until we are fit only to lie on the ground in frustration and bitterness.

Many of us are beginning to ask when improving ourselves by trying harder and running faster becomes, in fact, a losing of our selves and our lives. When we have discovered, molded, slimmed, bought, and fought our way to the point of externally perceived "perfection," what of us is left? A marvelous letter from a woman in Toledo says it all: "I've absolutely had it with being told how fantastic I can be. What about how fantastic I *am*?"

Life has been given to each of us as time that can be used to allow that "fantastic" person within us to come out and come true. It invites us to come out even on days when we don't look or act fantastic by the world's standards, and on days when we hurt or are scared, and on days when we don't think we'll ever be up to trying again. On those days life spends time on the lessons we need to learn about allowing others to be there for us and about the interconnectedness of us all.

Those who use life as a race in which one must pause only long enough to see who is gaining and what to wear for the victory ceremony are doomed to reach its end only to find that it seemed to be over before it really began.

But for those who discover how to live life as a journey in which there are not only races but slow walks and long talks and surprises around each corner, the fact that it may end at any moment really doesn't matter because the time lived will have been enough.

9
Making Choices and Letting Go

"You Can Have It All"

I think I was about seventeen or eighteen the first time I heard my father say, "You can't have everything."

I don't remember what the occasion was—probably some high school disappointment of mine that he tried to remedy with this annoying maxim—but all it did was show me clearly that once again he didn't "understand." On the one hand I was being told the world was mine if I just worked hard enough, and on the other I was being told I couldn't have it all. By the time I was 22 the words had become particularly bothersome to me, by the time I was 30 I couldn't stand to hear them, and by 40 I was out to prove them wrong!

A few years later I'd done it. I had it all: a career I'd fashioned myself, a long-term marriage to the same man, three attractive children nearing adulthood, a variety of interesting and interested friends, a string of publications to my name, and the opportunity in my work to travel all over the country, appear on national television, and get my share of standing ovations. I'd conquered depression and shyness and fear of flying. I even managed to give some pretty fantastic parties and to take ballet lessons again and get my Christmas cards out on time. I rejected the laughable notion that I was trying to be "superwoman." Hey, this was me, pure me, and I could handle it.

So what if my calendar had no free spaces on it for the next six months, that a spontaneous lunch with a friend was a memory, that clients could rarely get an appointment, that I hadn't read a book for fun in years, that the canoe hadn't been in the water all summer, that sometimes I didn't have time to unwrap the clothes I'd bought with the money I was working so hard to earn? What difference did it make that work consumed most of my waking hours and that I was tired most of the time? *I had it all!*

I was, in fact, so busy that it was only grudgingly that, on a brilliant day in May, I squeezed in my annual physical between a consultation in St. Louis and another in Columbus. A biopsy followed the physical, a diagnosis of breast cancer followed the biopsy, a mastectomy followed the diagnosis, and then, during my recuperation, a massive windstorm tore giant trees from our riverbank and flung them, along with power lines, against our house and flooded our basement. Then came a break-in of our house and the breakdown of a friendship that had been very important to me.

During this time when so much loss was juxtaposed against what my life had been, I first began to understand the wisdom of my father's words, and it was in the months and years that followed that I have been able to see clearly for the first time that the fullness of our lives has nothing to do with how much we cram into them and everything to do with making choices and letting go.

Expectation Exhaustion

Today's newspaper story and television ad and yesterday's best-seller tell us of yet another woman who is living her life as I once did. Tomorrow's article and next week's workshop will show still more women how they, too, can have it all. Here I read of a real estate saleswoman who has made over $10 million in sales by working twenty hour days, skipping breakfast and lunch, and turning her children over to others to care for temporarily so that she could work not full time but all the time. I pick up a book that tells me that I can, indeed, have everything and an ad that shows me a mug I should drink from because it will announce to the world what a busy, efficient, and fantastic woman I am every moment of my life. I see a notice that a doctor will discuss "modern woman and the many roles [sic] she plays." A television actress, being interviewed on a morning show, marvels at how her life has improved since she has come to realize that "the world is mine," and even as I write this there is someone somewhere writing an article about how, with just a slight adjustment in your calendar and vitamins, you can gobble up the world.

　　　　Exactly what do the words "having it all" really mean? First, there is the definition of the words "all" and "everything." What *is* "all"? What constitutes "everything"? A magazine article about women juggling motherhood and career says that men have long since learned that "having it all" can be attained by devoting full time to their job and turning over the care of the home and the raising of children to their wives. Fine—unless being with your family and having significant input into raising your children or having time for anything but your job is important to you, and then, if you follow this formula, the whole paradigm breaks down. Does "all" include health? What about fun? What about relationships? Mornings after? Feelings? Does "everything" mean all the money you want, no more worries, the perfect house, the perfect car, the ideal husband, the right number of chidren who never spit up or fall down? Is my "all" really the same as your "all," and if it isn't, who out there are we going to let define it for us?

　　　　For the thousands of women who have written and talked with me—and, I suspect, for millions more—figuring this out has been one of the most painful tasks of their lives. Knowing they don't want to go back to having nothing, yet seeing that going ahead seems to mean that one must be able to handle having it all, they are caught in a frightening ambivalence.

For the past two years I've been conducting a survey of women, asking them what they think is the biggest problem facing women today. The nearly three hundred women I've spoken with have ranged in age from 25 through 66 and come from all parts of the country. Some are full-time homemakers, most manage both home and job. Almost without exception (now a startling 92 percent) they say the biggest problem facing women today is that they have so many options that they feel guilty because they aren't "doing it all."

"I know I should be able to have it all," a housewife who is also an artist said. "But sometimes I just don't feel up to what it takes."

This woman, and many others like her, have found that their sense of self-worth has been savaged by what I call *expectation exhaustion.* Many women say that just watching the strong, "all-together" women on television makes them feel inadequate to meet the challenge of being "today's woman"; others say they feel so overwhelmed by the choices available to them that they seem to "grind to a halt." Some are experiencing yet another version of the new depression as the sense of loss at not being able to keep up overwhelms them. A woman in her mid-thirties who works as a petroleum engineer says that she used to feel happy with her life but now there are "too many voices, too many choices" telling her that she's not.

Women have to be very strong to withstand this barrage of voices and choices and the expectation exhaustion that they can engender. The expectations of others, coupled with our own expectations for ourselves, dissatisfaction with what we've had in the past, the natural human desire for the good things in life, and the daily confrontation with the news that all these good things are ours for the taking combine to lure us into the race. If we believe that "having it all" is to be taken literally and worked for accordingly, the race more often than not will end in our physical or psychic exhaustion, which has as its bottom line, "Where did it all go wrong?"

Until you realize that the only real "expert" in your life is you, you will be at the mercy of everyone you meet, every word that you read, and everything that comes across your line of vision. You will feel tense about falling behind, insecure about whether you are "doing it right," terrified that you might fail, unhappy with your looks, anxious about not having it all, and unsure of your own happiness even when it comes right up and sits in your lap and puts its arm around you.

Making Choices

It took a long time for the sun to go down that day, and the night which followed took even longer.

I had come to the hospital, the night of my breast biopsy, well accustomed to making choices in my life, but my choice-making had always before stopped short at the hospital admitting desk. Once I had put my street clothes in the locker, divested myself of my jewelry, and put on my hospital gown, I had always before given over not only my body but presumably my mind and spirit to the "experts." I had felt somehow that if I intervened in any way in this process of "healing," the whole procedure might go amiss, with disastrous results. Never mind that unfortunate results had already occurred to me in medical settings without my intervention: my belief in the power of patient passivity remained.

Yet here in front of me lay this surgical permission form, which would give my surgeon carte blanche on my chest the next morning. As I looked out my hospital window at the midnight pines, I knew sleeping pills could not blot out the fact that tomorrow was going to be a day which would call upon all the courage I could muster and which needed, tonight, my input into the preparation for it.

The decision to refuse to sign the permission for the one-step procedure (mastectomy to be performed immediately after the biopsy if cancer was found) was a hard one for me to make, given a belief in law, order, peace, and quiet in hospital settings. The nurse had told me hours earlier that my surgeon had left and could not be disturbed. I was alone. It was dark and it was late, and there was no "expert" with whom I could discuss my feelings of not wanting to do this thing in one step because of the need I felt for more time to think things through if the outcome was what I feared. I was frightened and angry and confused, but as I began to allow myself to relax and to pray, I was gradually moved to a certainty that I had never felt before: I knew that if there had been one hundred "experts" at my bedside, it would still have to be my decision to make there in the dark. I knew I needed my rest, I knew that the surgeon would not be pleased with my decision not to sign the permission form, and worse, I knew that this was neither his nor the hospital's treatment of choice. But I also knew it was the decision I had to make. I rang for the nurse.

From that night was born the strength I needed to face the morning's surgery and the diagnosis of cancer which followed, the capacity to think through what had happened and was going to happen, and the ability to make something redemptive of the entire experience. My choice, on that May night, to listen to my body, mind, and spirit and to allow myself to feel my connection with all that is eternal helped me to understand for the first time what healing and wholeness really mean.

The words "healing" and "whole" are part of one another: they share Old English roots. They speak of integrity and centeredness. They are not the province exclusively, or even mainly, of medicine. They are words that describe what our lives are to be about in their entirety and what they can be about if we are willing to do the hard work of making choices.

Balancing Your Life

A friend of mine tells me that she's always been fairly well satisfied with her clothing, but now that she's had a color analysis done she is beginning to doubt her own ability to choose anything in life without a "swatch." A graduate student says that her diet went "completely crazy" over spring break because she wasn't able to check it with her diet counselor. When I asked her if she couldn't have monitored it herself for the five days, she looked at me as if I had suggested she write her thesis over the weekend. Another woman is devastated when an interior designer tells her that her grandmother's tea cart, among other things, will have to go if she is to have the living room in her townhouse "she always wanted." She despairs of its loss because she and her husband use it for late evening suppers by the fire. Why then, I ask, doesn't she keep it?

"Because the designer said it had to go," she explained.

Making choices is hard, especially when you move into areas that are sensitive or problematical for you. It is tempting, with all the voices out there, to listen to them and let them do the hard work of choosing. But beware! Each time you let someone else live your life for you (which you do when you give them the power of making your choices), you loosen once again the connection you have with the person you were born to be. Each time you abstain from making a choice, you weaken yourself slightly so that the next choice and the next and the next become harder and harder to make. If you continue to do this, you can move yourself into depression because, once again, you will have lost touch with the life spirit within you.

Although the making of choices involves the use of our mind, body, and spirit, it's not quite that simple. Spirit, body, and mind *are* being "used" by the very fact that we are alive. Our task is that of recognizing and honoring each of these parts of ourselves and listening to them when they speak to us. They can be remarkable allies, and yet each can also be a powerful adversary if we don't give it the attention for which it is asking. An unused mind drifts into lethargy; an unattended mind is unable to bring to life any clarity of thought or speech. An unused body weakens, and an unattended one brings us into illness. To ignore one's spirit is to commit suicide on our life force itself.

But if the living of life is frequently problematical, the figuring out how to live it can be even more so! Five years ago I began teaching Life Balancing Workshops for women, in which participants learn to trust themselves in decision making, goal setting, and choosing when they want and need to eat, sleep, and play. In each group are women who want to move beyond using other people's answers yet are frustrated by having been told that the answers lie within them.

"I've tried to find them," they often say, "but I just can't seem to come up with anything."

In working with these women I help them see that finding answers and making choices in life is less a matter of trying than of allowing. I remind them that most little children have no trouble staying in tune with what they need, and I help them to allow themselves to reunite with the child that is within them, all the while staying in the maturity of the adult woman they have become.

Life Balancing is not a matter of jumping on yet another "stress and spirituality" bandwagon on the basis of someone else's perception that your mind and body are disaster areas or that you are fresh out of spirit. What the process does involve is (1) a recognition and affirmation that these parts of yourself exist, (2) practice in allowing them to speak to you and allowing yourself to listen, and (3) trust in the process and in yourself.

1. Recognition and Affirmation That Mind–Body–Spirit Exist

The gestalt of mind–body–spirit is so complex that to separate them, even for the purpose of this discussion, is to fly in the face of what wholeness is all about. Yet I am going to oversimplify and discuss *mind* as that part of ourselves which thinks, reasons, and contains our memories; *body* as our physical being; and *spirit* as the activating life force that drives us always toward our essence (who we were created to be).

Over the years I have found that almost every woman feels that one or two of these parts of herself is inferior to the other(s). Some women believe, for example, that the rational mind is the only part of themselves that should "control" what they do; others say they feel so "stupid" that they don't trust their minds. Many women say they believe the body is inferior to mind, and when it acts up by gaining weight, getting tired, or producing aches and pains, their remedy is to laugh it off, forget it, or drug it. Other women are uncomfortable with the word "spirit" because they are not accustomed to talking about it. Many of them forget that not too long ago the mind was also thought to be an unfathomable morass containing material best left unexamined, and they do not realize, until we discuss it, that science and spirit are coming ever closer in their embrace of one another.

By means of the Myers-Briggs Type Indicator, Isabel Briggs Myers shows us that some people are, by nature, more intuitive than others. Some respond to life more by thinking and others by feeling, some are extroverts and some introverts. Unless you know this, you may find yourself discounting your judgment or your ability to feel because it seems, in the situation in which you find yourself, "different" from that of those around you. You may try to negate your actions under the mistaken notion that there is a "better" way to be, or you may—as I once did—discount your intuition because you heard somewhere that it was not a reliable guide to behavioral direction. When you do any of these things, you throw yourself off balance and weaken your ability to make the choices that are right for you.

My experience with breast cancer exemplifies how recognizing, accessing, and trusting the resources of our body, spirit, and mind are necessary in choice making:

- My choice of a two-stage procedure would have been foolhardy had I not known and considered the risks inherent in a second round of anesthesia before deciding that they were outweighed by my need to have time to think over what was happening to me.

- My remembrance that I do better in decision-making times and hurting times without big crowds around me prompted me to ask for a "No Visitors" sign.

- My sense that people appreciate those who show strength in hospitals lost out to my remembrance that in times of fear my body needs copious amounts of touching and comfort. This allowed me to swallow my pride and ask for all the hugging and hand-holding anyone could spare and for my teddy bear to be at my side at all times.

- My remembrance of unpleasant experiences in large hospitals fought with my knowledge of the capabilities large medical centers offer, but my decision was to stay in the more healing atmosphere of my hometown hospital. (However, my need to be a participant in my choice of treatment impelled me to ask for the opinions of specialists from those larger research centers concerning treatment.)

- Knowing that I prefer truth to avoidance, I chose, against the warnings of others, to look at "after" pictures in medical journals before my mastectomy and to ask that my husband be with me when the dressings were removed. Looking at those pictures, which were no more "frightening" than looking at pictures of an eleven-year-old girl, and seeing my husband's benign reaction, gave me the courage to correct those who wanted to commiserate with me over my "disfigurement."

- My choice of a mastectomy instead of other options was made on the basis of reading I'd done and my trust in my surgeon and his opinion.

- My lifelong need to recover in my own time and at my own pace emboldened me months later to announce to family and friends that I was going to sit out the holidays that first year.

When our choices are made, as these were, with integrity on our part, they are good choices. This does not mean that the results will always be perfect—or even right—but they will be good because they are based on the most authentic choices we could make. It is also important to note that my choices were mine alone and would not necessarily have been right for anyone else.

To make authentic choices in life we must go to our *mind* (What are the facts? What can I read to learn more about this? What is the reality of the situation? How have I reacted in similar situations in the past? Were those reasons valid? What can and can't my surgeon/auto mechanic/accountant/doorman do? What will or won't my boss/lawyer/ secretary/child/friend do? What might happen if I choose this?), our *body* (What is my body trying to tell me now? What does it feel like right now? How do I usually feel when I'm alone, tired, in a crowd, excited, jealous? What coping strategies work for me? What would feel good to me now? What will I feel like if I choose this?), and our *spirit* (Which, of the alternatives open to me, is most in keeping with who I really am?)

For many of us, the integral part of making choices is the "allowing" prayer, in which we become aware of our connection with the eternal. Without forceful petition, without demanding an answer, we allow ourselves to wait there until we feel a sense of being led and supported in our choice making.

2. Practice in Listening to Mind–Body–Spirit

In the Life Balancing Workshops I help women to see that this is not a mysterious process that can be managed by some but not by others. As they feel, smell, and then taste freshly cut apples, for example, they become aware of how full attention to a single piece of food on their plate can enhance its taste and the pleasure they get from eating it. They see that by stopping before each meal to let their bodies tell them what they want, they can avoid many of the diet pitfalls into which they have previously fallen. Some women have discovered, as have I, that plain food can often produce such beautifully pungent flavors that eating simply is not a punishment but a joy. The occasional feast then becomes unalloyed pleasure rather than a round of guilt. Women also discover that when their body is crying for a certain type of food—even if that food is a no-no—they had better pay attention to it because it means something. Sometimes it means that they need to obey the cry and eat the candy bar or the steak or seek out the frosty mug. Other times, as we have seen, the hunger is for something other than food, and attention must be paid.

Women who are bothered by insomnia have learned that going to bed by the clock without taking into consideration what their bodies want is counterproductive. Others have learned that taking a nap in the middle of the day, if they are tired, or canceling something to stay home to rest is not morally reprehensible but an appropriate response to the body's call for rest. They also learn to distinguish between physical tiredness and mental fatigue and how, through relaxation techniques, to create rest periods even during nonstop days of work.

Fern, a woman in her sixties, was typical of many women in discovering that her spirit seemed smothered under her sense of obligation to others and her belief that "moms don't need fun." It was only when she discovered this during a Life Balancing Workshop and began to allow herself time to play (she did this by resuming the square dancing she'd always loved, by taking a day off once a month to visit a friend in the next town, and by allowing herself to be "silly" once in a while) that she began to feel, as she said, "like myself again." (The old expression "feeling like yourself again" is, incidentally, an absolutely accurate appraisal of what healing and wholeness are all about.)

JoAnn, a mother of five children under ten, saw in a Life Balancing Workshop that it was her mind that was starving. A philosophy major in college, she rarely read anything anymore except the daily paper. She took tranquilizers occasionally and said she felt she was becoming "unglued." After the workshop, JoAnn enrolled in an Egyptology discussion group one night a week at her suburban library. She now looks forward to the meetings and to reading at least a few hours each week. She describes her experience this way: "Before, I just kept saying I was too tired or didn't have the time or couldn't leave the kids with a sitter or blah-blah-blah, until the excuses became part of the problem. I finally saw while I was in the workshop that I was spending as much time crying about not having time to read as I would spend if I took the same time and *did* it. . . . The first meeting I sat there like a clod, but by the third time I was right in the discussion. It feels so good to know my brain isn't dead."

Diane, a psychologist with few free spaces on her calendar, tried out for a role in a musical comedy produced by a little theater because, as a woman who loves to sing, she was beginning to feel severe imbalance in her life. The role, although time-consuming, reenergized her because it put her back in touch with parts of herself that had been hungry for expression.

3. Trusting in Process and Self

Several years ago a geologist friend of mine left her work to do what she had always wanted to do: open a stained-glass studio. Just shows, I thought when I heard about it, why women don't get ahead. No staying power. But when I saw Rowena recently I began to understand. This was no copout, no backing out because of "fear of success." This was an authentic response to a felt call from her very being—her life force—and by her answering it she became more whole than she had ever been. Fully aware of the financial risk she was taking and the hard work that lay ahead as a freelance artist, she was nevertheless vibrant and more fully alive than I had ever known her to be.

Rowena had trusted the process and herself in the face of much that was scary and unknown. Could I, as a teacher of this process, do less? Although I had trusted the process and used it in my life for several years, when it came time for me to make a decision about my doctoral studies, my courage wavered. The obvious choice given my career path was a Ph.D. in marriage and family counseling at a major university. Yet from the moment I mailed in my application I began to feel a dull ache that started in the pit of my stomach and moved throughout my body until it became a burden to lift my arms or to move my feet one in front of the other. Pushing aside what I knew was happening, I pretended it was "just the flu"—a disease that gets the blame for many of our mistakes! After two weeks I realized that my body and my spirit were not going to quit talking until I stopped rationalizing and began to listen.

Only after I did what I had long felt called to do—applied for entrance into a doctor of ministry program in spiritual counseling—did I feel my body relax and my life resume its balance. Paper career paths do not always fit real live human beings, I have found, any more than paper goals make dreams come true.

Making choices does not mean that we have to have all of the answers. It does not mean that we must stop attending classes, reading books, or consulting friends, color analysts, diet counselors, physicians, attorneys, or interior designers. What it does mean is that in this thing called life we have been named the contractors and although we may enlist as many subcontractors as we like to help us along the way, we are responsible for the job.

Letting Go

I had come to the hospital, that day before my biopsy, somewhat accustomed to making choices, but I had not fully realized that the other side of choice making is letting go. I had come, in fact, with armloudfuls of life, impatient at this delay and eager to get on with my collection of things and experiences that would nail down the happiness and security of my life.

But the events of the weeks and months that followed that experience were not about collection and security: they were about loss—of a part of my body, of the belief that I would live forever or even my normal life span, of the configuration of our property, of the security of our home, and of a valued relationship. From each of these losses I learned important lessons.

The lessons were not immediately apparent to me. I rejected, for example, the one suggested to me by some: "If you work too hard, you'll get sick." That seemed too shallow to consider. Instead, because of my

own lack of energy and my own need to take space and time for myself, I allowed the lessons to come to me in their own way and in
their own time.

In our fascination with choice making, we often lose sight of the
fact that the other side of choice is letting go. If we drive the interstate,
we cannot stop to buy raspberries at the little stand on the bypass. If I
marry Sam today, I probably can't go out to dinner with Ben tonight. If I
stay home with my children, I won't be at my career peak in fifteen years,
but if I leave them in a day-care center now, I won't have a headful of
memories of their growing-up years when I'm retired. Letting go is intrinsic in choice making, but no one talks much about it because it appears,
at first glance, to be a sort of leftover second best.

But as I began to live more and more with the idea of letting go,
I found that because it has a marvelous energy of its own, it does not
have to take second place. There is intrinsic in the act of relinquishment
a feeling of great freedom, and this freedom in turn allows us not only to
accept further loss without becoming devastated but actually to seek out
further chances to let go. From a person who had always surrounded
herself with a bastion of things and people and then held on to them
very tightly lest I lose any of them, I became a person who began very
purposefully to let go. Instead of going through life with clenched fists,
holding tightly to my life and all that "I" had put in it, I began to unclench
my fists, open my palms, and let go. At first with disbelief but increasingly with assurance, I realized that an open palm can not only let things
go but is at all times open to receive the new things life has to offer. As I
began to let go of addictions, possessions, the need always to be right, I
began to discuss these possibilities with others.

As they began to see that the subtle balance of making choices
and letting go produced richness in their own lives, they began to share
their stories with me. For example, Nell, a middle-aged minister long
caught in her need to do both Sunday sermon and three-course Sunday
dinner, saw how letting go of this unrealistic agenda was a loving move
since it had been done more to feed her own guilt than to feed her family. Guilt can be the authentic response we feel to an action for which we
are sorry, but it can also be a distorted pride stance. *Letting go of inauthentic guilt* can free both ourselves and others.

There is also tremendous freedom to be found in *letting go of
the belief that we are responsible for another's happiness.* Margaret

thought that if she could just find the right words, she could make her two daughters happy. One, she said, had a marriage that was in trouble, and the other "works too hard and has no time for men." Although we can support and love others, each of us has our hands quite full enough with the task of living out our own happiness. To presume that you can do that job for others is to doom yourself to a task that will be chronically frustrating to you (as Margaret found) and continually annoying to those you are trying to manipulate into being happy (as Margaret's daughters found).

Letting go of the need to be perfect is often a move that frees not only you but all of those with whom you come in contact. Beryl's family—husband and two daughters—had all suffered from her insistence that there was only one right way to do everything. Only when chronic bronchitis and other physical problems plagued both daughters and her marriage came to the edge of divorce did Beryl agree to seek the counseling she needed to help her see that perfection is not something that humans are able to achieve. By making choices for herself that were in tune with who she is (she likes a neat house, a well-dressed family), while letting go of the idealized self-image she had (perfectly clean house, no messy clothes ever, sit-down meals three times a day), Beryl was able to maintain her integrity without destroying that of those with whom she lives.

Letting go can also be tremendously helpful when your calendar is so full it rises up from your desk and grabs you by the throat. After several nights of watching me run from room to room in a panic of exhaustion as I prepared for another speaking trip, my husband helped me learn how to let go of obligations. The procedure works like this: Fighting back my natural desire to take control, I let go by taking a few moments to sit down and breathe deeply so as to center myself. I then go to my calendar, look at the next few days, and choose one or two of the most important events. Then I announce loudly and clearly to myself—and anyone else within earshot—that I am not going to do——, ——, and —— (all the remaining items). At this point, since I am on the edge of exhaustion, I take the time to get in touch with what I need, and then I give it to myself. This can be an immediate bath and bed, or it can be calling up friends to go out to play. It can be eating or fasting or sitting and staring. It can be playing the piano or crayoning (a very relaxing pastime my older daughter recently introduced me to), or it can be biking or walking. This process produces a lessening of pressure, which, more often than not, allows me later in the week to do the very things I had said I was giving up and allows me to do them feeling relaxed and invigorated. Embarrassingly simple as this process sounds, it has gotten me through everything from keynote addresses to book chapters to abdominal surgery and lots of things in between.

But the most valuable lesson I learned from the events of the summer of loss of which I have written is that we can *let go of things and of people.* Once I began to understand this reality I began to allow myself purposefully to let go. Because in my work I frequently have to live away from home in a small motel room for a month at a time, I began to decide, while packing, just what things I really do need to be "happy." The list was refreshingly small! In my own home I then began to examine seriously just what things I really need to enjoy life and what things are just filling up space. I began to appreciate why I have always loved the openness of my living room with its high-beamed ceiling and white walls and furniture, and why I rejected a decorator's decree that it needed more this or that. I began to understand the joy I have always felt about a single, beautiful *anything* and why I've alway preferred two days at the best possible place to two weeks of too much. I began to see that I did not have to own something to enjoy it and that, in fact, the owning of it more often than not curtails some of the joy because I then have to deal with its upkeep and "dailiness."

Two years ago my husband and I very intentionally decided to require ourselves to throw out one thing for every new thing that we buy. From the time we made that decision, we found that our delight in buying and owning has sharpened immensely. A colleague who has come to a similar decision about her own life told me that since shopping has always been and still is one of her greatest pleasures, she responds to her need to buy things by giving them to others rather than feeling that she has to take all of them into her own nest as she once did.

I once thought that people, too, had to be "mine" or I could not really enjoy them. Unless we talked on the phone once a week and lunched together every other, and unless we declared our exclusivity and sat next to each other whenever we met, our relationship had obviously soured. Only within the past few years have I found that the most satisfying interpersonal moments with old friends—and with people I have just met—are those which are unplanned, unexpected, unstructured, and unfettered. The open palm, which releases others from the prison of our need for them, is also the life that is open enough to enjoy the variety of people we meet on our way through it. Letting go of the preconceived notion of the kind of person we "need" to be with or "should" know, or the kind who "will accept us," frees us to enjoy the fullness of life that comes from wholehearted interaction with it.

In the summer of the year of loss of which I've written, I bought a license plate that says VIVO—"I live." This is not, as some have thought, the brash shout of someone who has, for the moment, outsmarted death. On the contrary, it is an awareness of both the joy and fragility of existence and a daily reminder to me of its beauty.

We cannot have it all. We cannot, as one of my former students told me at a party recently, "have the whole cake." That we can is a cruel myth and, when you think about it, a dumb one. Who really wants it all?

It is only when we recognize "having it all" for the buzzwords they are that we can go on to live out our own definition of them. The hard, stubborn, and immovable fact is that while there is a gorgeous smorgasbord out there from which to select, a wise person knows that she must survey the whole thing and then summon the courage to make choices and the grace to let go.

10

Living Your Happy Ending

It is easy to lie with words, but very hard to lie with pictures. The picture of the woman on my desk does not lie.

It is a picture of me on vacation in Wyoming with my husband, and we are in the Snowy Range between Cheyenne and Laramie. Behind us are gray, craggy cliffs streaked with snow remnants and a mountain lake bordered with pines. Above is a sky that stretches forever, getting more blue as it goes.

I look at myself and I like what I see—a woman who looks happy about where she is and who she is. Even though we are on a high range, as I look at the picture I am reminded of the words of the Shaker song:

'Tis a gift to be simple
'tis a gift to be free
'tis a gift to come down
    where you ought to be
And when we find ourselves
    in the place just right
'Twill be in the valley of love
    and delight.

My journey to this place—both the mountain and the valley—
has been made up of so many pieces, so common and so singular and
so momentous and so inconsequential. The struggles and the suc-
cesses are a patchwork, shredded in places by events so painful that
they seemed ready to tear it all apart, but overall rich in color and texture.

As I look again at the picture, I see reminders of choices I made
in the face of warnings and advice from others: On my T-shirt is the
name of a company that makes jeans. It is also my first name, one I created for myself many years ago out of my first initial, my husband's first
initial, and that of our first child because my own name had never felt
right to me. I remember the puzzled confusion that followed my announcement of this change, and I remember the night a man sputtered
at me in front of a large group at a reception, "Only insecure women
and movie stars change their first names." In the picture I am wearing
the contact lenses I got ten years ago. I still recall struggling not to cry
when the young technician sneered, "What are you, some kind of weekend swinger? You'll never be able to stand these at your age." My ears
are pierced several times ("Trying to be a gypsy?"), and my hair is
straight with bangs ("It doesn't look professional"). The shoes I have on
in the picture remind me that I bought them the time my son flew to
Boston to spend the weekend with me. We flew kites all that Easter
weekend instead of sightseeing. ("You mean your son came to Boston
and you didn't take him to see Old Ironsides?")

My journey spills over and mixes in memory with the journeys of
the women I've known and worked with and taught and loved and with
whom I've shared so many hours these past years: Jerry and Susan, of
whom I've written, who learned that our talents can free rather than im-

prison us, and Betty, Pauline, and Carol who learned that happy marriages are not based on textbooks or fairy tales but on the reality of two
human lives. Claire, who discovered, with so many of us, that power has
more to do with intrinsics than extrinsics, and Marianne and Carola, who
learned that by accommodating you can become stronger and freer
than ever before in your life.

I think, too, of the other women I've known who've learned that
the journey to happiness is not a curving arc but a series of jagged lines
that often pierce one's heart in the process but, in their cutting, can also
free one's spirit. Among them:

> Annette, who went from thinking her life was over at 23 to
> turning her skill at weaving into a business that takes her to
> shows all over the country

> Margot, who moved from severe depression through two years
> of therapy and on past her doctorate to become an outstanding
> East Coast therapist specializing in the needs of depressed
> women

> Karin, who got over her fear of flying and went to Israel, the land
> of her birth, and Nan, who went alone to seek her roots in
> Yugoslavia

> Donnelle, who at 52 realized that she had as many answers as
> anyone and, after nine children and thirty-two years as a
> housewife, took the Women Helping Women Peer Counselor
> Training and is now a human services administrator

> Jan, who came to realize that an angry husband leaving without
> saying goodbye did not have to "disintegrate her into
> nothingness"

> Marie, who very purposefully gave up her career in the theater to
> devote full time to having and raising four children

> Nora, who at age 43 was left by her husband with three children,
> no money, and no job skills but can now write that she has
> "three grown children who are doing well and a great job which
> pays me more than I ever expected to earn"

Bernice, who cared enough about herself to take some heavy critique on her appearance and her self-presentation and change them to where she can say "I was born at age 57"

Colette, who said the hell with it when they said she'd never walk or talk again after a stroke and is now not only walking and talking but working as a paraprofessional counselor in a hospital

Norma, who, hating her southern roots and feeling dumb because she had never graduated from high school, earned her diploma and went on to start a new career in the state she'd left in defeat as a teenager

Randi, 23, who, though she's had all the feelings of being a trapped housewife, says she has decided not to have them anymore! She loves canoeing, skiing, walking in the rain, laughing, writing poetry, reading, riding on the back of a motorcycle with the wind in her hair, needlepoint, people, and life, and "doesn't want to wake up seven years from now and find I haven't danced!"

What can we learn from all this? Are we just a random group of women who were lucky enough to stumble into happiness? Or are there some common threads here that we can trace to get a clearer picture of what happy endings can really be about?

I believe very strongly that there are common threads, and I have, in these pages, written of many of them. The threads are not simple, monochromatic do's and don't's, and they never will be, because life is not one-dimensional. The threads are multicolored strands that often tangle in paradox. We must, for example, develop our independence even as we acknowledge that we are interdependent with all other human beings and all else in creation. We must continue to learn and read and ask, all the while knowing that we ourselves are the ultimate experts for our own lives. We must be willing to affirm the already written scenarios of others even as we go about the lonely task of writing and living our own. Even when we feel so tired of trying we are ready to take anyone else's script for an answer, we must resist the temptation, whether it beckons us into marriage, the office, the boardroom, or the birthing room.

We must learn to walk the fantastically fragile line between advance and retreat, between giving in and standing our own ground. We must be patient enough with our own impatience to allow the ebb and flow of life to enter by whatever means without grabbing it by the nape of the neck or slamming the door in its face because it doesn't seem to make sense. We need always to allow our lives to balance themselves, not by force, but by our enabling of our body, mind, and spirit.

We must at some point, if we are to live, take the time to define who we are, trust ourselves to make decisions for our lives, and then act them out. We must understand that by doing this we will not have ridden off into Pollyanna City free forever from pain and loneliness, because intrinsic in our choice making is letting go. But, knowing all this, we must still approach life with our arms outstretched, ready at any moment to dance or play or do a cartwheel. Even as we understand that moments—and life—do not last, we must open ourselves to each of them fully or we will never catch even a glimpse of what happiness is all about.

As I write this the phone rings and a friend is on the line. We talk awhile before she tells this story:

"I went to the airport to pick up a friend. When he arrived he said I looked wonderful and then he asked me if I was happy. I paused for a long time, but then, since he is a person who expects answers to his questions, I finally had to give him one.

"'Yes,' I finally said. And then more strongly, 'Yes.'"

I asked her what she thought the pause had been about, what had been going through her mind.

"I just kept thinking, 'How can you be happy when you have so much to do?' and 'How can you be happy when so many other people aren't?' But then I realized, darn it, I *am* happy, and so I said it."

As I finish the final paragraphs of this book, I think about that phone call. It reinforces the sense I've had for over a year of the evolution that is taking place in the way women handle the happiness that does—or doesn't—come into their lives.

For so many years women's answer to "How are you?" has been "Fine" and to "Are you happy?" has been a quick affirmative. Since one had "obviously" achieved one's happy ending—husband, home, and children—to answer otherwise was to admit defeat. Only a fool or an ingrate wouldn't be happy when she had "everything." To say more would have required saying too much.

But women have now been presented with a new vision of what a happy ending is supposed to be about. Now it is the woman who admits she *is* happy who often feels foolish and out of step. With so much to do, to achieve, to conquer, and with so much unhappiness out there, who among us can afford to be something so trivial as happy? When we get caught up with our work and get our bodies perfectly sculpted and maybe get nominated for president, then maybe we can allow ourselves a little happiness. But meantime . . .

Where once the boundaries of what was said to constitute our happy ending were so circumscribed by home and hearth that sometimes our spirits shriveled, now the horizon has become so remote that we hardly dare rest and enjoy along the way. Where once we were told that our cocoon would have to go to allow the butterfly in us to emerge, now the butterfly often circles in frustration as new vistas open daily to beckon us on even though our wings are not up to or interested in making the trip.

A vision of happiness that is so narrowly defined that it hampers the spirit is not good, but neither is one that daily recedes farther into the unattainable distance. Both breed fear, doubt, and, because they trigger feelings of loss, more depression. A vision of happiness in which the goal becomes more important than the journey is one that makes us a prisoner of expectations.

It is only when we understand that happiness is not something out there which is given to us by others as a reward for something we have done that we can break free from this prison. It is only when we realize that our happy ending has more to do with embracing present moments than it does with collecting a gold watch at the end that we can begin at last to live it every day of our lives.

References

Benson, Herbert, M.D. *The Relaxation Response.* New York: William Morrow &
    Co., 1976.

Bolles, Richard Nelson. *What Color Is Your Parachute?* Berkeley, Calif.: Ten-
    Speed Press, 1983.

Frisbie, Richard P. *How to Peel a Sour Grape: An Impractical Guide to Success-
    ful Failure.* New York: Sheed & Ward, 1965.

Fromm, Erich. *Man for Himself.* New York: Rinehart, 1947.

Henry, O. "The Gift of the Magi." *Best Stories of O. Henry.* Garden City, N.Y.: Sun
    Dial Press, 1945.

Holland, J. L. *Making Vocational Choices: A Theory of Careers.* Englewood
    Cliffs, N.J.: Prentice-Hall, 1973.

Keyes, Ken Jr. *Handbook to Higher Consciousness.* St. Mary, Kentucky: Living
    Love Publications, 1975.

Kirsten, Grace, and Richard Robertiello, M.D. *Big You Little You: How to Bring
    Yourself Up All Over Again Using Separation Therapy.* New York: Dial
    Press, 1977.

Kopp, Sheldon. *If You Meet the Buddha on the Road, Kill Him!* Palo Alto, Calif.:
    Science & Behavior Books, 1972.

Lao-tzu, *Tao Te Ching.* From *The Tao: The Sacred Way,* ed. Tolbert McCarroll.
    New York: The Crossroad Publishing Co., 1982.

Lederer, William J., and Dr. Don D. Jackson. *The Mirages of Marriage.* New
    York: W. W. Norton Co., 1968.

LeShan, Lawrence. *How to Meditate.* Boston: Little, Brown, 1974. New York: Bantam Books, 1975 (paperback).

Maitland, David. *Against the Grain: Coming through Mid-Life Crises.* New York: Pilgrim Press, 1981.

May, Rollo. *Power and Innocence.* New York: Dell, 1972.

Myers, I. B. *Manual: The Myers-Briggs Type Indicator.* Palo Alto Consulting Psychologists Press, 1975.

Ross, Alan. *Learning Disability: The Unrealized Potential.* New York: McGraw-Hill, 1977.

Tillich, Paul. *Morality and Beyond.* New York: Harper & Row, 1963.

Index

A

accommodation, 11–12
  as conflict management, 116–118
  as decision, 115–116
  as fact of life, 112–114
  as meditation, 119–123
  as reconciliation, 123–125
  versus "settling," 114–115
achievement, 128
Against the Grain: Coming through Mid-Life Crises, 32
agoraphobia, 130
ambivalence, 3–4
anger, 107, 108, 123, 124

B

balance:
  need for, 52, 65–66, 78, 139–140
  planning for, 140–144
Benson, Herbert
Bettelheim, Bruno, 93, 94
biological time clock, 3

Bolles, Richard, 27
boredom, in jobs, 24, 25

C

calendar, as aid to life balancing, 140–144
cancer, 136, 155
career counseling, 27
caring for others, 11, 21
Center for Women's Alternatives, 85
child care, 44
child rearing, 42–45; *see also* parent-child relationship
choices:
  and depression, 10
  exhaustion from too many, 149–151
  learning to make, 151–161
  letting go of, 159–163
  and self esteem, 93, 94
  for women today, 2, 6, 145
commitments, and life balancing, 143

communication, *see* interpersonal
    communication
conflict management, and
    accommodation, 116–118
contracts in marriage, 47
counseling, *see* career counseling,
    group counseling, mental
    health counseling

D

"death trip" as aid to life balancing,
    142
"decade answers" to happiness, 6
decision-making, 100–101
    and accommodation, 115–116
defining-deciding-doing paradigm,
    97
depression, 51–68
    avoidance of through options, 10
    biochemistry of, 59
diet, and mental health, 61, 62, 136,
    157
doing (taking action), 101–103
drug abuse, 53, 60
dyslexia, 80

E

exercise, to treat depression, 61, 136
expectations:
    exhaustion from, 149–151
    for interpersonal communication,
        73–75
    for happiness, 5–13
    in marriage, 36–42
    others', 144–145
    for personal looks, 132

F

failure, and depression, 57
fantasy, as aid to life balancing, 142

fifty-fifty marriage, 46–48
forgiveness, *see* reconciliation
friends, 45
Frisbie, Richard, 29

G

goals:
    and job search, 26–27
    setting, 138, 139
group counseling, 86–88
guilt, 28, 29, 92, 93, 101, 160

H

happiness:
    decade answers to, 6
    expectations of, 5–7, 8–13
    failure to attain, 2, 4
    jobs and, 17–19
    journey to, 167–170
    see also success
"having it all" expectation, 12–13,
        148, 149–150
healing imagery, 136
Holland, J. L., 75
housewife, role of, 35, 36
    and depression, 55–56, 57, 58
housework, 3, 20, 22–24
How to Meditate, 122
*How to Peel a Sour Grape: An
    Impractical Guide to Successful
    Failure,* 29

I

*If You Meet the Buddha on the Road,
    Kill Him!,* 108
illness, psychological aspects of,
        101, 136
inadequacy, feelings of, 129, 130,
        133
input overload, 138

insomnia, 157
interdependence, 49
interpersonal communication:
  and accommodation, 117
  and happiness, 11
  and marital sacrifice, 40, 41
  methods to facilitate, 77–82
  women, men's expectations for, 73–75
  women, men's patterns of, 75–76
interview procedures, 27
intuition, 154

J

Jackson, Don D., 82
job priorities, 25
job upgrade, 27
jobs, 15–32
  as expectation for happiness, 9, 13, 17–19
  and no-talent trap, 24–28
  and talent trap, 28–32
  see also working women

K

Kopps, Sheldon, 108

L

learning disabilities, 76, 80
Learning Disability: The Unrealized Potential, 80
Lederer, William, 82
LeShan, Lawrence, 122
letting go of choices, 159–163
life balancing, 139–144
  and making choices, 153, 155–156
Life Balancing Workshops, 153, 156, 157

loss, 159
  as trigger of depression, 10, 57

M

Maitland, David, 32
marriage and family, 33–50
  communication in, 71–84
  expectations toward, 36, 37, 45, 46
  and happiness, 7–8, 10, 13
marriage-enrichment, 11, 70, 81
mastectomy, 148
meditation, 137, 142
  accommodation as, 119–123
menopause, 61
mental health counseling, 61
mind-body-spirit, 153, 154–158
The Mirages of Marriage, 82
mother-daughter relationship, 82, 83
Myers, Isabel, 154
Myers-Briggs Type Indicator, 154

N

1970's decade, changes in, 8
non-accommodation, 11–12
No-Talent Trap in employment, 24–28
nurturing trap, 35

O

obligations, letting go of, 161

P

parent-child relationship, 82–84, 108
Passages, 55
perceived external value (PEV) activities, 143

perfection as a goal, 57, 145, 161
personal looks, 130–132
personal power, 104–106, 107, 108
    and accommodation, 114
play, need for, 66–68, 136, 157

R

reality concept for working women,
    20–24
reconciliation, 123–125
recreation, *see* play
relationships:
    trying to correct within marriage,
        45, 46
    communication in, 11, 71–84
    reconciliation in, 123–125
    and sacrifice, 40, 41
relaxation, 62, 141–142
The Relaxation Response, 62
resumés, 26, 27
Ross, Alan, 80
rural life, 53–55, 99

S

sacrifice, 39, 40, 41, 53
self:
    search for, 63–64, 94–103
    trusting in, 158–159
self definition, 96–100
self-esteem, 92–94, 96, 104–106
    and accommodation, 114, 115
settling versus accommodation,
    114–115
Shaker song, 166

"shoulds" and "ought to," 29, 93,
    139; *see also* guilt
silence, value of, 88–90
spirit, denial of and depression, 63;
    see also mind-body-spirit
Spock, Benjamin, 55
staying home; *see* marriage and
    family
suburban lifestyle, 55–56, 99
success, 5; *see also* happiness

T

Taft, Sue, 31
Talent Trap in jobs, 28–32
talking it out, *see* interpersonal
    communication
time management, 138–144
Tobin, Joe, 68
"try harder" syndrome, 12, 133–138

V

value-intrinsic activities (VI), 143

W

Wet Towel Reality Probe, 21–24, 46,
    77
What Color Is Your Parachute?, 27
Women Helping Women, 15, 21, 72,
    75, 91, 134
work, to treat depression, 63
working women:
    and depression, 57, 58
    see also jobs